Boko Haram

OHIO SHORT HISTORIES OF AFRICA

This series of Ohio Short Histories of Africa is meant for those who are looking for a brief but lively introduction to a wide range of topics in African history, politics, and biography, written by some of the leading experts in their fields.

Boko Haram

Brandon Kendhammer
and
Carmen McCain

OHIO UNIVERSITY PRESS

ATHENS

Ohio University Press, Athens, Ohio 45701
ohioswallow.com
© 2018 by Ohio University Press
All rights reserved

Printed in the United States of America
Ohio University Press books are printed on acid-free paper ⊗ ™

28 27 26 25 24 23 22 21 20 19 18   5 4 3 2 1

Library of Congress Cataloging-in-Publication Data
Names: Kendhammer, Brandon, author. | McCain, Carmen, author.
Title: Boko Haram / Brandon Kendhammer and Carmen McCain.
Other titles: Ohio short histories of Africa.
Description: Athens, Ohio : Ohio University Press, 2018. | Series: Ohio short
histories of Africa | Includes bibliographical references and index.
Identifiers: LCCN 2018031924| ISBN 9780821423516 (pb : alk. paper) |
ISBN 9780821446577 (pdf)
Subjects: LCSH: Boko Haram--History. | Terrorist organizations--Nigeria,
Northern--History--21st century. | Terrorism--Prevention--Government
policy--Nigeria. | Social conflict--Nigeria, Northern--Religious aspects.
| Nigeria, Northern--Social conditions--21st century. | Nigeria--Politics
and government--21st century.
Classification: LCC HV6433.N62 B6535 2018 |
DDC 363.3250966909051--dc23
LC record available at https://lccn.loc.gov/2018031924

Contents

Illustrations

Figures

Maps

Acknowledgments

Thank you to Gill Berchowitz of Ohio University Press for her tireless support and encouragement of this project. We also thank the two anonymous reviewers for their feedback and suggestions. Over the years, we have both accumulated substantial debts in the form of support and encouragement, and we cannot thank everyone here. Nonetheless, we wish to especially acknowledge Cornell University's Institute for Africa Development, the University of Vermont Rakin Lecture series, and the Northwestern University Nollywood Working Group, who hosted presentations of this work in draft form. We are also grateful to Philip Ostien, who provided invaluable primary sources on Boko Haram's early days, and to the communities of Kannywood filmmakers and Jos-based music video producers who were generous with their work responding to and influenced by the conflict. We dedicate this book to the lives of all of Boko Haram's victims, and to the remarkable courage of so many Nigerians affected by its violence.

Map 1. Nigeria. *Map by Brian Edward Balsley, GISP*

Map 2. Northeastern Nigeria. *Map by Brian Edward Balsley, GISP*

Introduction

In July 2009, a showdown was brewing in Maiduguri, northeastern Nigeria's largest city. On one side were the followers of a charismatic local Muslim scholar named Mohammed Yusuf. Yusuf had risen over the course of a decade from relative anonymity to become one of the most influential (and radical) clerics in the country, building a community of thousands of followers informally known around the region as "Boko Haram" (roughly, "Westernization Is Forbidden"). A powerful public speaker and skilled organizer, Yusuf taught that Nigerian Muslims had fallen away from the "true" Islam of the Prophet's time and that it could only be restored by rejecting outside influences such as democracy and Western-style education. To that end, he and his supporters had amassed money, property, and (it was rumored) weapons in anticipation of a showdown with a government they regarded as entirely illegitimate.[1]

On the other side were fearful local authorities, many of whom had watched Yusuf's rise with interest and even sought to co-opt or collaborate with him on their own political schemes in the years following

Nigeria's surprising return to democratic rule in 1999. In recent months, they had responded to growing evidence of his strength and rumored connections to more violent movements in North Africa and the Middle East by stepping up their campaign of public harassment and intimidation, and the situation was clearly escalating. It would take only a little spark to set off an explosion.

On July 26, Yusuf's supporters struck first, and the police and military responded with their full might. Within just a few days, eight hundred members of the group were dead, many reportedly killed in cold blood by security forces after the fighting had stopped. The tally included Yusuf himself, illegally executed behind a police station after interrogation. Soon after, the Nigerian government declared the movement over and the problem solved. Yet within a year, Boko Haram had rebuilt itself under the leadership of a charismatic and vicious figure named Abubakar Shekau, Yusuf's former second-in-command. Under Shekau, Boko Haram fashioned itself into a violent jihadist movement dedicated to destroying the Nigerian state and establishing its own strident vision of Islam as the law of the land. Within just a few years, it would become one of the deadliest insurgencies in the world, capable of mounting well-planned bombings, brutal hit-and-run attacks and assassinations, and even winning pitched battles with the Nigerian Army.

Yet for the vast majority of Nigerians, the realities of the war—and by 2013 it was indeed a war, with a federal state of emergency in three of Nigeria's thirty-six states and a massive troop deployment—made little impression. Nigeria's political leadership downplayed the conflict's severity, both to its own people and the international community. Meanwhile, rumors (partially true but often wildly exaggerated) that the group was supported by foreigners circulated as proof that Boko Haram was not really a *Nigerian* problem after all but a local affair for Muslims "up there" to solve.

Even after nearly a decade of conflict that has displaced more than two million people, killed tens of thousands of civilians, and opened up a massive new front in the "global war on terror," the conflict's geographic isolation to one of the country's poorest corners has left many Nigerians deeply alienated from the war in their midst. And although the broader global public has occasionally caught glimpses of this conflict, it remains poorly understood and underreported. The result has been nothing less than a massive and complex catastrophe that, as of this writing, affects millions of people across the Lake Chad Basin region, even as politicians in Abuja (Nigeria's capital) and international officials debate potential courses of action and struggle to provide security and assistance to some of the most vulnerable people in the world.

In part, this book is the story of Boko Haram as a movement and the violence it has perpetrated. But it is also a *social* history that examines the conflict in northeastern Nigeria as a phenomenon much larger than a single terrorist group and its actions. We have chosen to tell this story because, as you will soon see, we view Boko Haram's rise and bloody career as not only a product of its religious vision but also a consequence of Nigeria's deep-seated social and political challenges. Understanding Boko Haram and the destruction it has wrought requires first understanding the local circumstances that gave rise to it and that have fed the conflict ever since.

A Tale of Two Countries

In 2013, a story in the British newspaper the *Guardian* reported that Nigeria was the second-fastest-growing market in the world for champagne.[2] When Nigeria makes the international news, it is often for this sort of human-interest narrative that points a bit too cleverly to the country's vast contradictions. The country is home not only to famous oil reserves (35 billion barrels as of 2017) but also to two of Africa's three wealthiest men (entrepreneurs Aliko Dangote and Mike Adenuga). For anyone who has spent time in the tonier parts of Lagos, Nigeria's 21-million-person megacity, or encountered wealthy Nigerians abroad, it is not hard to believe that this rapidly growing country of 180 million citizens is an increasingly profitable market for luxury goods.

In recent years, Nigeria's wealthy reputation has become one of its most visible exports. Everything from a 2016 documentary called *Lagos to London: Britain's New Super-Rich* to a recent "Kleptocracy Tour" of London highlighting suspiciously expensive real estate owned by Nigerian politicians paints an admittedly not particularly flattering picture of a nation in ascendance. And, indeed, at least some Nigerians see this extravagance as an opportunity. Since 2009, when Nigeria's Ministry of Information launched a notorious "rebranding" campaign designed to change the country's international image, the government's goal has been to repackage it as an up-and-coming power, deflecting attention away from the corruption and poverty that remain major problems in the lives of ordinary citizens.

This new Nigerian image—a country that dominates international music and film charts, hosts powerhouse media and fashion industries, and is a hub of investment and financing for technological innovation—is true, and it reflects improvements in the lives of many Nigerians. But it also obscures other, harder realities. Nigeria is the only large country in the world that has seen an *increase* in the number of people living in extreme poverty since 1990, and, although it returned to civilian rule in 1999, the promise of (as many Nigerians put it) a "democratic dividend" paid off to ordinary, working-class people in the form of better government and greater attention to issues of social justice has not arrived.

What does this inequality look like? Lagos's glamour hides massive slums such as Makoko, where hundreds of thousands live in ramshackle houses built on stilts in the city's lagoon. And the country's inadequate infrastructure means that even middle-class Nigerians struggle to obtain services such as electricity and safe, affordable transportation, while the poor lack necessities such as clean water and health care. In the Niger Delta, home to the country's oil reserves, activists and militants have fought a decades-long battle with the federal government, demanding their "fair share" of the resources that have brought the country billions while polluting their air and ground. And in the country's Muslim-majority north, there is a long history of religious scholars and activists using the language of Islam to challenge corruption, poor governance, and a lack of social justice.

The idea that the Nigerian story is a "tale of two countries" is not new. Chinua Achebe used it in his 1987 novel *Anthills of the Savannah,* which depicts a fictional West African country called Kangan (a loose stand-in for Nigeria) deeply divided between its capital's wealth and cosmopolitanism and the poverty and neglect of its interior. But many Nigerians (and a fair number of outsiders) see the most important division between Nigerians as civilizational, pitting an increasingly prosperous majority-Christian "south" against a "backward" Muslim-majority north. The two halves of what we call Nigeria today—brought together by colonial fiat in 1914—do have important and durable differences in terms of culture and language, in how they were governed by their colonial rulers, and (to some extent) in their levels of prosperity today. These differences are real, and they have played a significant role in shaping the country's legacy of ethnic and religious conflict.

But are they inevitable and unresolvable? Many Nigerians still agree with the legendary politician Obafemi Awolowo, who wrote that Nigeria was a country without a nation, a "mere geographic expression." For his part, Achebe, in his final book in 2012, *There Was a Country,* revealed that he had come to see the country's pained history of violence and civil war in civilizational terms, describing his own ethnic group (the Igbo) as naturally open to cultural change and progress, while Muslims from the Hausa and Fulani ethnic groups (collectively the majority in northern Nigeria) are "hindered by a wary religion" and their desire for domination.[3]

But if there are really two Nigerias, these simplistic and reductive accounts do not do either of them justice. For one, they mask the many ways in which Nigeria's economic, political, and social interconnectedness transcends religious and ethnic differences. For another, in Nigeria, corruption and its benefits know no particular ethnic or religious boundaries, a fact that has often made it harder, rather than easier, to build coalitions to address the country's biggest challenges. And, finally, they fail to recognize just how much the citizens of any country, whatever their differences, share a common fate. Sooner or later, a crisis for some Nigerians becomes a crisis for all.

The Stolen Girls

Unofficially, Boko Haram became a "crisis for all" on the night of April 14, 2014, in the sleepy town of Chibok, roughly 120 kilometers south of Maiduguri. There, members of Boko Haram stormed the compound of a girls' secondary school, reportedly looking for building supplies. What they found instead were hundreds of young women who had recently returned from a break to take their final examinations. Despite rumors of an impending attack, government forces had been slow to provide additional security, so when the assailants arrived they encountered almost no resistance. In all, they kidnapped 276 students that night, girls who aspired to become doctors and nurses, teachers and scientists. Although "the Chibok girls," as they would come to be known, were hardly Boko Haram's first victims, their fate quickly became a symbol at home and abroad of the struggles and violence faced by many ordinary Nigerians living in the shadow of their country's prosperity.

This kidnapping was only the most recent tragedy in a community that had suffered more than its share. The town takes its name from the local hills where its residents once fled to escape from slave raiders sent by powerful local kingdoms, who roamed the region until the late nineteenth century. More recently, as a Christian-majority enclave of roughly sixty thousand citizens in a state home to nearly six million, Chibok's residents have often faced inattention or even marginalization from local authorities. Not that there was much to go around: Borno State and its neighbors in the northeastern region suffer from some of the highest rates of poverty, illiteracy, and child and maternal health risks in all of Nigeria.

Soon after the attack, there was a surge in international interest in Boko Haram, accompanied by new efforts to explain the group's motives, goals, and place in the world of global terrorism. Much of it depicted the group's actions first and foremost as an attack on girls and their access to education. American celebrities such Angelina Jolie, George Clooney, and (perhaps most famously) Michelle Obama promoted the #BringBackOurGirls hashtag, originally begun on Twitter by Nigerians, as a vehicle for drawing attention to the female victims of religious extremism around the world. Another similar narrative emphasized the role of poverty and a lack of education in driving extremist violence in places like northeastern Nigeria. After all, what better evidence of the link between poverty, ignorance, and violence than a group of radical extremists in one of the poorest parts of the world who declared "Western education" forbidden by God and kidnapped girls who attempted to access it?

Unfortunately, this outrage did little to stem the tide of violence. At best, stories like the Chibok kidnapping can lead to globally organized movements that lobby governments and international agencies. At worst, sensationalist international media coverage actively detracts from the work of local organizers, whose appeals are drowned out by the megaphone of what the Nigerian American writer Teju Cole has referred to as the "White-Savior Industrial Complex." However well-intentioned, this global activism has had very little real on-the-ground impact on either Boko Haram or Nigerian policy toward the conflict. And while Boko Haram's victims have certainly drawn less attention internationally than those of attacks in cities such as Paris, Brussels, San Bernardino, and Istanbul (to name only a few), it is not a lack of press coverage that allowed the group to kill more than twelve thousand civilians and displace 2.6 million from their homes and communities from 2010 to 2017.

Boko Haram as a Nigerian Story

Chibok and its aftermath are essential to the Boko Haram story, but one of our goals is to take you beyond those headlines and into a deeper understanding of the conflict's origins and its consequences for the millions of ordinary Nigerians caught in the crosshairs. Cutting through a tangled web of evidence, we hope to offer a clear and concise story about who the members of Boko Haram are, where they came from, how they have operated, and the toll they have taken on the ordinary Nigerians (and Cameroonians, Chadians, and Nigeriens) in their path.

More broadly, we hope that the book will help readers understand how the story of the "two Nigerias"—one wealthy and globalized, the other poor and insecure—has influenced both Boko Haram's emergence and the Nigerian government's tragically ineffective response to it. Certainly, it is important to acknowledge Boko Haram's place in a larger global story about the rise of jihadist terror and insurgency in the early twenty-first century. But we also argue that the group's history, rise, and (hopefully) fall are deeply connected to this Nigerian story, in which a country of great wealth and opportunity nonetheless found itself confronting one of the world's deadliest insurgencies.

In the hands of the country's ruling class, a simplistic version of the "two Nigerias" story emphasizing the inevitability of conflict over the country's ethnic and religious differences helped nurture the conditions that made Boko Haram possible. Yet, as we hope to show, a more nuanced understanding of how inequality, injustice, and poor governance unite many Nigerians across lines of ethnic and religious identity also reveals how the struggle against Boko Haram has brought out the country's best. Beyond discussions of Boko Haram's history, ideology, and tactics, this book aims to tell stories about how a wide range of Nigerians—particularly artists, writers, and musicians—have responded to the crisis, often in ways that bring Nigerians together rather than pushing them further apart.

* * * *

As of this writing, the story of Boko Haram and the fight against it remains unfinished. Although the Nigerian government has repeatedly declared them "technically defeated," they continue to kill. Millions of residents of northeastern Nigeria (and across the Lake Chad Basin) are unable to return to their homes and begin the long process of rebuilding their communities, while others are terrorized (and, increasingly, taxed for revenue to sustain the insurgency) by members of the ISIS-affiliated "Islamic State in West Africa," a Boko Haram offshoot that split with Shekau in 2016. Some but not all of the Chibok girls have been released from captivity following negotiations between the government and leaders of the Boko Haram faction that held them, and protesters continue to challenge government's inability to free the thousands of other captives who remain. Meanwhile, new abductions and suicide bombings have continued with depressing frequency. Although events may eventually overtake some of the details we offer here, we hope that this book provides a useful marker along the way to what will surely be more comprehensive histories in the years to come.

1

A Nigerian Origin Story

Boko Haram's origins are shadowy and poorly understood. Even after nearly a decade in the limelight, most
of its leaders—dead and alive—remain ciphers. The
record of its creation and consolidation is filled with
speculation, pseudonyms, and peripheral characters,
and even credible sources differ on the specifics. But for
all intents and purposes, the *crisis* of Boko Haram began
in 2003 in the village of Kanama, in rural Yobe State just
south of Nigeria's long border with Niger.

Here a small group of Muslims (estimates range
from about fifty to several hundred) angry about the
sinfulness of Nigerian society attempted to withdraw
from it. Their haphazard collection of tents and mud-
brick houses were objects of bemusement to locals, who
referred to them as the "Hijra Group" in reference to
the *hijra*, the flight of the Prophet Mohammed from
Mecca to Medina in 622 CE. They called themselves Al-
Sunna Wal Jamma (People of the Prophet's Example),
a name that highlighted their relationship with Salafism, a global Islamic ideology that seeks to "purify" the
faith by returning to the example of the Prophet (the

sunnah) and the earliest Muslim community. Although Salafi movements are often seen as products of the Arab world, Nigerian Salafi preachers and organizations are among the most influential in Africa.

Globally, Salafis are divided about how their religious values ought to relate to the political world. Some use politics to establish their vision of a good society, while others (the so-called quietists) focus on promoting personal piety and religious education. Still others—a minority but a vocal one—see modern governments as beyond reform, justifying violent struggle against them. Initially, the very nature of the Hijra Group's action—physical and symbolic retreat from Nigerian society—seemed to put it among the quietists. But the speed with which it turned to violence suggests that its members were divided over how to achieve their goals.

The Hijra Group's actions were undoubtedly influenced by grievances it shared with many Nigerian Muslims. In 1999, following the inauguration of Nigeria's first elected government in a generation, a handful of politicians in the northwestern state of Zamfara announced their intention to implement a strict version of shari'ah (Islamic law) in criminal law, with the goal of restoring it to the status it held prior to colonial rule. The subsequent outpouring of popular support turned the "shari'ah issue" into a movement, and between 1999 and 2003, twelve states enacted shari'ah-inspired legislation and policies that were met with high hopes by Muslim citizens.

A minority of Muslims clearly hoped that Zamfara's proposal would be the first step in moving the country toward an Islamic theocracy. This possibility was also on the minds of Nigeria's 85 million Christians (the country has a roughly equal proportion of Muslims and Christians), and the two religious communities clashed repeatedly over the next decade. For most Muslims, however, shari'ah's popularity was rooted in the hope it might force Nigeria's notoriously corrupt political class to address their demands for economic development, social justice, and political rights. Yet, whether because the benefits rarely materialized or because punishments for the wealthy and well-connected never seemed to equal those imposed on the poor and vulnerable, public opinion on shari'ah quickly soured. This letdown was especially crushing for the Salafi activists who had set aside their discomfort with formal politics in the hope of influencing the process. For them, shari'ah's failure was an outright betrayal.

In Kanama, the Hijra Group and local citizens lived alongside each other peacefully for months. Locals reported that members occasionally took on farm labor jobs to earn money, but mostly they kept to themselves. Things unraveled in late 2003 when the group's use of a fishing pond came to the attention of a local chief, whose request for an access fee was met with anger. Tempers rose, and the police got involved. On December 20, several members were arrested, and others were beaten and harassed. There is confusion about what happened next.

Some point to provocations by local authorities, others to threats by group members against the local government chairman and the district head, the ranking local agents of the Nigerian state. On December 24, the group stormed a nearby police barracks and overpowered its defenses, killing at least one policeman and coming away with a cache of arms. From there, it raided the town of Geidam, gathered more guns, and prepared for war. By early January 2004, it had made its way overland 250 kilometers to the Yobe State capital of Damaturu, all the while engaged in a series of running battles with the police. Here it was dispersed but only after sacking yet more police stations and reloading its armory.

Over the next few days, police and military forces ramped up operations that claimed dozens of perpetrator deaths and arrests. There were also indications of the conflict's mounting social costs, as ten thousand people fled their homes and farms during the fighting. It was also around this time that the name "Nigerian Taliban" appeared as the group's "official" moniker. Some journalists claimed that they had seen fighters flying a Taliban flag, while others referenced a shadowy leader nicknamed "Mullah Omar" after the Afghan jihadist. However tenuous, the "Taliban" narrative grabbed the public's imagination, driving the first global media coverage of the violence and kicking the interest of international intelligence agencies into high gear.

The first wave of attacks ended shortly after Damaturu. A month later, the police produced a man named

Sheikh Muhiddeen Abdullahi, who was announced as the group's mastermind and primary funder. Abdullahi was Sudanese and had worked in Nigeria as a representative of Al Muntada, an international Islamic charity based in London with ties to Saudi donors and a history of rumored (but mostly unsubstantiated) connections to terrorist groups. Subsequent inquiries found scant evidence of any direct involvement but some that Al Muntada had sponsored mosques in which Hijra Group (and later Boko Haram) members preached. While security forces followed up Abdullahi's arrest with a declaration of victory, he was never tried and was later quietly released.

In September 2004, the "Taliban" reemerged near Bama and Gwoza in Borno State on the Cameroon border. Once again, they targeted police stations and were pursued by federal forces who announced inflated death counts following a series of indecisive engagements. By this time, authorities had also identified one of the group's main leaders, a man named Muhammad Ali (sometimes Alli), a former student at the Islamic University of Khartoum and a Maiduguri native. In 2014, the International Crisis Group (ICG) issued a bombshell report that linked Ali to Osama bin Laden, whose February 2003 audio message had declared Nigeria to be one of the most "qualified regions for liberation" by jihad.[1] Based on interviews with alleged Boko Haram participants (and later confirmed in its broad strokes by correspondence recovered by US forces during the raid that killed Osama bin Laden), the ICG claimed that in 2002 Ali returned to Nigeria with $3 million from bin Laden's organization as "seed money" to establish an al-Qaeda cell.

Among the recipients of this funding, the ICG suggested, was a local Salafi cleric named Mohammed Yusuf. Yusuf was well known for both his preaching and his relationship with Sheikh Ja'afar Mahmoud Adam, arguably the most prominent Salafi thinker in Nigeria at the time. Yusuf was not at Kanama during the conflict, and his personal connections to those who were remain a matter of speculation. We do know that he preached at the Alhaji Mohammed Ndimi Mosque in Maiduguri, where Ali and some of the other Hijra Group members worshipped. Eventually some former members of the "Taliban" fell back into Yusuf's orbit, part of a new movement eventually known as the Yusufiyya.[2]

Ali was most likely killed during or shortly after the events at Kanama. The remaining members scattered during an October 2004 artillery barrage on their hideouts along the Cameroon border, and after that little was heard of them. Local authorities were eager for the story to die down, and state security agencies alternated between taking credit for "crushing" the group and avoiding any explanation of how they had allowed it to emerge in the first place. For the moment, peace returned.

What Boko Haram Is—and Is Not

With Boko Haram rated in 2015 by the Global Terrorism Index as the world's deadliest terrorist organization, there has been no shortage of explanations for its bloody success. Three are especially important. First, as part of a region—the Sahel—considered one of the world's poorest and most vulnerable, northern Nigeria has poverty and weak governance that, many argue, make it especially susceptible to extremist violence. Second, security analysts and policymakers immersed in the global war on terror tend to see the group's rise through a global lens, with special attention to its connections (some shadowy, others more public) to groups such as al-Qaeda and the Islamic State of Iraq and Syria (ISIS), to which a portion of the group first pledged allegiance in March 2015. Third, local Nigerian conspiracy theories about Boko Haram's under-the-table sponsorship by politicians and military men have circulated for years, part of an effort to place the group's actions within accepted local notions of how Nigerian politics "works" and who wields "real" power.

What is the truth? Research on the causes of violent extremism finds that simple stories rarely capture the complexities behind how terrorist organizations emerge, recruit, and operate. Take poverty, for example. If poverty were a key driver of violence, Nigeria would be a likely candidate. In 2012, Nigeria's National Bureau of Statistics reported that over 60 percent of its citizens lived on less than a dollar a day. And despite more than $600 billion in oil revenue since 1960, many Nigerians lack access to basic social services and infrastructure, such as a steady supply of electricity, safe roads, and effective law enforcement. In the northeast, the story is even bleaker. There the poverty rate was upward of 75 percent before the conflict, and no one is certain how much worse it has gotten. Primary school attendance rates are half those in the rest of the country, and so are average incomes. Childhood vaccination rates hover around 10 percent, and nearly a quarter of children suffered from symptoms of chronic malnutrition even before the conflict. It is not surprising that many domestic and international observers identity the region's economic circumstances as a key source of Boko Haram's strength.

The most visible symbol of these challenges are the ten million children—the *almajirai*—sent away from home to study in informal schools where they memorize the Qur'an and learn the basics of Islamic theology. Although almajirai are technically the responsibility of their parents and teachers, many live in the most extreme poverty. And, indeed, many leading Nigerian public figures, most famously Nobel laureate Wole Soyinka, have argued that the almajirai are especially vulnerable to radicalization.

But although this relationship might seem obvious, a growing body of research casts a skeptical light on a simple or straightforward relationship between poverty and terrorism. Not only are the poorest countries around the world *not* especially likely to suffer from terrorist attacks, but individuals in extreme poverty are not particularly likely to join or even support terrorist groups. Indeed, a surprisingly high proportion of the members of groups such as al-Qaeda and ISIS have university and postgraduate educations, particularly in fields such as engineering and medicine. Reports in the aftermath of the Hijra Group's wild ride suggested that some of its members hailed from the wealthiest families in the region.

These findings line up with what we know about Boko Haram's efforts to recruit supporters and fighters. From its earliest days, the group has marketed itself as a friend to the poor, targeting young men and families in need of welfare assistance and even extending small business loans to youths willing to aid the cause. Yet researchers who have spoken with former members have found that those who took Boko Haram up on its offers often saw themselves as economically equal to or even better off than their friends and neighbors who resisted.[3] In Nigeria as elsewhere, the poorest of the poor do not have a monopoly on feelings of disenfranchisement or a lack of opportunity.

These findings also hold up in the case of the almajirai. The anthropologist Hannah Hoechner has found that for many Muslims, becoming an *almajiri* is less a choice of poverty and desperation than it might seem. Hoechner's interviews with with almajirai and their parents find that many of the families who send their children to these schools distrust Western-style, government-run education—and for good reason, given its poor quality.[4] What limited face-to-face information we have from former fighters confirms that while some alma-jirai have joined Boko Haram, they make up a small percentage of the group's membership.[5] The idea of a radicalization pipeline running directly from Qur'anic schools into Boko Haram's clutches is a myth.

There are similar problems with the "international influences" story. To be sure, transnational Islamic extremist groups such as al-Qaeda and ISIS have clearly attempted to both influence and take credit for Boko Haram's rise. Aside from bin Laden's 2003 declaration that Nigeria was ripe for jihad and the alleged seed money he provided to Mohammed Ali, documents recovered from the al-Qaeda chief's compound in 2011 suggest that Boko Haram's leadership had reached out to him as early as 2009. By the early 2010s, US and Nigerian intelligence reports suggest that al-Qaeda in the Islamic Maghreb (AQIM) was providing tangible support, particularly in the form of training members who traveled to camps in AQIM-occupied territory during the 2012–13 crisis in northern Mali. Soon after, both Boko Haram and Ansaru, an AQIM-affiliated Boko Haram offshoot, ramped up efforts to kidnap and ransom Westerners, one of AQIM's signature tactics. Similarly, many observers have noted a marked change in the style of Boko Haram's videos following its allegiance with ISIS, suggesting that ISIS's media affairs personnel had pushed it to adopt their "house style."

Although international influences have indeed shaped Boko Haram, this line of argument also tends to disguise the fact that Boko Haram's goals and actions are mostly shaped by local conditions. Indeed, the group has repeatedly demonstrated an ability to attack the weaknesses of local police and military forces and shift in the face of their strengths. For example, the group followed reports of low troop morale and mutiny in military barracks in the spring of 2014 with an aggressive offensive to take and hold territory, while in the face of an international troop "surge" in spring 2015 it shifted back to terrorism, launching a suicide campaign that used an unprecedented number of women and girls as bombers.

It is also misleading to assume that Boko Haram's evolution must have required major outside guidance. For one, it overstates the technical difficulties involved. As we will discuss in more detail later, Yusuf, Shekau, and others in the group's leadership did try to seek out contact with al-Qaeda in the group's early years. However, there is little evidence that these efforts translated into much direct assistance.

What is much clearer is that the group has consistently benefited from the extraordinary mismanagement that has ravaged the Nigerian security services. Indeed, senior military and defense officials stand accused of misappropriating more than $5.5 billion allocated to the fight against Boko Haram in the mid-2010s and failing to prevent the widespread abuse of civilians in military custody. Both have played a key role in Boko Haram's success. For another, it also neglects the fact that many of Boko Haram's most effective tactics, especially its large-scale kidnappings of women and girls and their subsequent deployment as bombers, are clearly not borrowed from the al-Qaeda/ISIS playbook. And although by 2016, military setbacks in ISIS's core Syrian and Iraqi holdings and internal politics within Boko Haram's leadership had driven some members of both groups into closer collaboration (particularly on matters of theology), evidence of direct military cooperation remains elusive.

Third, debates within Nigeria about the "real" causes of Boko Haram reflect broader tensions around the balance of national power that have dominated Nigerian politics since before independence. Since the 1999 transition, Nigeria's political stability has depended on an informal agreement that presidential power would "rotate" between the Christian-majority south and the Muslim-majority north. Following the unexpected death in 2010 of President Umaru Musa Yar'Adua, a northern Muslim who had not yet completed the first of his two allowable terms, Vice President Goodluck Jonathan, an evangelical Christian from the southern Niger Delta region, became president. Jonathan's campaign (and eventual victory) for his own term in 2011 was deeply controversial, with Muslim leaders pressuring him to step aside in favor of another Muslim. But despite the fact that Boko Haram had emerged before the public eye under Yar'Adua's watch in 2009, its campaign of violence provided ample fodder for conspiracy theorists to cast its activities in terms of Jonathan's presidency and the "marginalization" of northern Nigeria.

Most of these theories focus on finding Boko Haram's political and military "sponsors," revolving around the idea that Boko Haram was either a product of the Muslim community's hatred of Jonathan or of Jonathan's own secret scheme to discredit his opponents. Given the stakes, it is easy to imagine that some members of Nigeria's political class have tried to sponsor or co-opt Boko Haram. Yet most accusations, such as the arrest of Borno senator Mohammed Ali Ndume in 2011 on accusations that he had been providing secret support to the group, turn out to have clear political motivations (Ndume had fallen out politically with the state governor) but little evidence. And as a number of Nigerian and international negotiating teams have discovered, governmental agency in-fighting and Boko Haram's own internal fragmentation are just as good an explanation for the failure of so many efforts to bargain with the group as the shadowy interference of political actors.

The truth is that from the very beginning, Yusuf and his followers were deeply involved in local politics. Members of his community were courted as political muscle and appointees and even rewarded financially in exchange for their support. For example, then Borno State gubernatorial candidate Ali Modu Sheriff not only reportedly recruited members of Yusuf's group as thugs during his 2003 election campaign but also sought out Yusuf's personal endorsement. Yet when these relationships soured, they fed disillusionment and resentment.

Where should we be looking to better understand Boko Haram? According to the Global Terrorism Index project, 92 percent of the world's terrorist attacks since 1989 have occurred in countries where the government is a major sponsor of violence against vulnerable communities.[6] Many Nigerians would surely contest the notion that northern Muslims are "vulnerable" when they have frequently held the country's highest political offices. However, it is possible to see the government's response to the Hijra Group and later Boko Haram as part of a disturbing and long-standing pattern of violence and repression against movements that seek, even quietly, to challenge the moral legitimacy of the powers that be.

A second factor is the role of religious ideology, particularly Salafi Islam. The question of when and how religious extremism leads to violence is a thorny one, and even good-faith efforts to "understand today's terrorists" can end up reducing complex debates to simplistic conclusions. Both globally and in Nigeria, the vast majority of Salafi-influenced Muslims reject violent struggle as the best path to achieving their goals. Yet even moderate Salafi doctrine often seems intolerant of alternative interpretations. It is impossible to understand Boko Haram's emergence without understanding a bit about the history of Nigerian Salafism and equally impossible to trace Boko Haram's integration into a system of "global jihad" without understanding the ideology behind it.

The Legacy of Islamic Dissent in Nigeria

The events of 2003–4 in Yobe and Borno followed a pattern that is immediately familiar to students of Islam in West Africa. For more than two hundred years, communities of Muslim dissidents inspired to preach religious revival and combat political injustice have been at the center of some of the most transformative social revolutions in African history. The most famous is the Sokoto Caliphate, founded in 1808–9 following Shehu[7] Usman dan Fodio's jihad against the local Hausa states. Today the caliphate's hereditary rulers—the sultan of Sokoto and the emirs of northern cities such as Kano, Zaria, and Bauchi—are both symbols of the region's Islamic heritage and important figures in their own right. The Shehu's jihad and its legacy loom large over the contemporary political and religious terrain, a powerful reminder of how a community of principled dissidents can transform society.

The Shehu's career has important parallels with the men who founded Boko Haram. Like many of them, the Shehu spent much of his youth in the region's vast religious educational system. The ideology he developed, which both predates modern Salafism yet shares with it a number of key concerns, was based around the problem of *bid'a* (usually translated as "innovation") in spiritual life. Bid'a is more than just an arcane theological issue. It represents the idea that as societies depart—even in small ways—from literal adherence to the Qur'an and the sunnah, they lose their morality and sense of justice.

39

For the Shehu, there was no better evidence of the problem of bid'a than life in the kingdom of Gobir, the most powerful state in what is now northwestern Nigeria.

Gobir's ruling elite had been Muslims for generations. But to the Shehu, they were apostates who flouted the laws of Allah, forced their subjects to pay heavy, un-Islamic taxes, and refused to enforce shari'ah. In 1794, he set off on his own hijra with a small group of followers. His new community, based in Degel (southwest of modern-day Sokoto), seemed to have little interest in fighting. Indeed, as historian Murray Last observes, it was rare in those days for religious revivalists to take up arms, and their students were more likely to wield sticks than swords in self-defense.[8] It was around this time that the Shehu began to see himself as a *mujaddid,* a once-in-a-generation reformer who paves the way for the arrival of the Mahdi, a redeemer who ushers in the end-time. This millenarian streak was an important part of the Shehu's popular appeal, and although the Mahdi never appeared, the idea that the end-time might be just over the horizon often reoccurs during moments of social crisis in Muslim-majority West Africa.

For another decade, the Shehu criticized Gobir's elite from a cautious distance, while they responded by banning his followers from wearing the veil and turban and even taking members of his family as hostages. After years of skirmishes and increasingly violent attacks on his followers, he declared his jihad in 1804, and, four years later, his army marched into Gobir's capital of Alkalawa as conquerors. By 1812, his flag-bearers had conquered the bulk of contemporary northern Nigeria, laying the groundwork for the Sokoto Caliphate, a state intended to govern in strict accordance with shari'ah.

The Shehu's movement provides many Nigerian Muslims with a clear model for how to create a just Islamic society. But where he succeeded in establishing a new political and religious order, most who have followed in his footsteps have not. Indeed, just as the Shehu struggled for a decade to build a movement in the face of a seemingly endless cycle of co-optation, confrontation, and repression, most Islamic dissenters across the region find themselves targeted by state authorities as dangerous threats to the status quo, threats to be nipped in the bud before they become revolutions. Speaking about his own strategy to combat another small community of Islamic dissenters known as Maitatsine some 170 years later, Nigerian military dictator (and future elected president) General Muhammadu Buhari said simply, "I flew into Adamawa [site of a major attack in 1984] as head of state, and that was the last you heard of Maitatsine." The fact that the operations he authorized—aerial bombardment, mortar fire, and high explosives against populated areas—destroyed thousands of homes and displaced thirty thousand civilians went conspicuously unacknowledged. Repression and violence have often thwarted the ambitions of Islamic dissent movements in northern Nigeria, but they have rarely killed them completely.

Another example of this pattern is the caliphate's conduct against its Muslim opponents. From its founding, critical voices feared that along with success might come political corruption and religious backsliding. Indeed, even the Shehu and his brother Abdullahi dan Fodio expressed doubts about whether their new system could live up to its idealism. Yet, despite these misgivings, the caliphate's leaders insisted on the fundamental rightness of their religious mission, going so far as to threaten other Muslims who challenged their monopolization of "true" Islam with military annihilation. This insistence was evident in the famous correspondence between the Shehu, his son Muhammad Bello, and Muhammad al-Kanami, a scholar and military commander of the Bornu Empire, situated to the caliphate's east in the Lake Chad Basin (and including much of Boko Haram's contemporary heartland). Facing pressure to join the jihad or be attacked by the Shehu's allies, al-Kanami drew on Bornu's eight-hundred-year history as a Muslim nation and his own scholarly prowess to challenge their claims that his empire had slipped away from true Islam and that the Shehu and his followers possessed universal religious authority over the region's Muslims. Although it was al-Kanami's military success that eventually beat back Sokoto, his arguments remain a powerful challenge to any Muslim ruler in the region attempting to enforce his own orthodoxy.

Nor did the challenges end after the Shehu's death in 1817. Bello's election as caliph triggered a massive

internal feud among some of the Shehu's oldest supporters, many of whom saw his quick move to consolidate
power (and control over the spoils of war) as violating
the collectivist spirit of the jihad. In response, Bello's
forces waged a "second jihad" against these domestic
enemies, one more markedly more violent and punitive
than the original. Sokoto's rulers never ceased to face
criticism that they were failing to live up to the Shehu's
standards—criticism that they often met with yet more
military campaigns against fellow believers.

With the caliphate's conquest by British forces in 1903,
the issue of religious dissent gained new stakes. The British
officially promised noninterference with Islam (a policy
that they repeatedly violated), but prominent Muslim
scholars organized violent resistance, assassinating colonial officials and staging small-scale uprisings. Others
proposed hijra to Mecca. Following his defeat, Caliph
Attahiru I (the Shehu's great-grandson) attempted the
journey, gathering tens of thousands of followers along
a winding road toward the east. Pursued by British
forces, they were slaughtered near the village of Burmi
in present-day Gombe State.

Those who stayed faced a barrage of movements
declaring the arrival of the Mahdi to wipe out the British invaders. The most threatening was headquartered
in the village of Satiru, just southwest of Sokoto. Led by
a blind preacher named Saybu dan Makafo, the Satiru
community included thousands of runaway slaves from
Sokoto's plantation economy. On March 10, 1906, they

faced off in a battle pitting 573 colonial riflemen and 3,000 Sokoto soldiers on the British side against 2,000 men armed with little more than farm implements. The result, which British officials called a "signal and over-whelming victory," was closer to a bloodbath.[9]

Even as Satiru marked the end of violent resistance, intellectuals warned of colonialism's impact on the moral fabric of society. Mallam Zum'atu al-Fallati, a Kano-born scholar who spent his life preaching across colonial West Africa, composed a series of poems in the 1940s and 1950s that attributed the region's growing spiritual malaise to the policies of British Christian rule. Mallam Zum'atu focused much of his ire on the "barracks" (in Hausa, *bariki*) established across the region to house British administrative and military authorities, which eventually became spaces where people excluded from "polite" Muslim society congregated. For Mallam Zum'atu, the barracks were symbolic spaces where the moral rules of Islam did not apply, a visible symptom of colonialism's consequences.[10] Today many "good" Muslims still see police and military installations as places where drinking, gambling, and prostitution flourish under the neglectful eye of political authorities.

Mallam Zum'atu also pointed to new Western-style schools (the first opened in Kano in 1908) as another pernicious influence. As linguist Paul Newman notes, the name "Boko Haram" reflects a local hundred-year-old debate about the moral status of secular education. Although many of the region's leading families embraced

44

Western-style education for their children, the newly built schools were often regarded with deep suspicion by religious leaders and commoners. While it is hard to tell from their contemporary reputation as little more than victims of poverty and child abuse, historically the almajirai were regarded as future productive members of society, training not only for their own moral edification but also to take on important and even prestigious roles as jurisprudents and educators. One estimate suggests that in the early twentieth century there were as many as twenty-five thousand Qur'anic schools educating almajirai in literacy in the *ajami* script in which both Arabic and the local languages of Hausa and Fulfulde (the language of the Fulani) were written.

With the advent of British-run schools and their adoption of English and a romanized script, tens of thousands of almajirai were effectively rendered officially illiterate. Perhaps not surprisingly then, many families impacted by this shift dismissed these new schools as *boko,* a word that conveyed the idea of fraud, inauthenticity, and deception. The term *karatun boko* (literally "writing of deception") eventually came to denote all Western-style education. While today millions of Nigerian Muslims attend these schools, popular skepticism about their value runs deep.[11]

After World War II, the advent of democratic elections reenergized Muslim dissenters, who focused their criticism on the remnants of the caliphate's ruling class (the *masu sarauta,* or "titleholding class") and the political party—the Northern Peoples' Congress (NPC)—they supported. The NPC's leader, Sir Ahmadu Bello, the *Sardauna* (captain of the bodyguard) of Sokoto and great-great-grandson of the Shehu, was a masterful politician who played heavily on his family heritage by flying Dan Fodio's banner at rallies and distributing posters of his auspicious family tree. But for critics such as the firebrand religious scholar and socialist Aminu Kano and his Northern Elements Progressive Congress (NEPU), the continued dominance of the masu sarauta had nothing to do with their piety. As Kano and his supporters saw it, whereas the Shehu had sought to stamp out autocratic government, Bello and his allies had used their heritage to monopolize power and maintain their privilege. But while NEPU's criticism gained them supporters, the NPC's control of the regional government gave it the ability to silence and marginalize their critics. In one particularly ignoble turn, the *waziri* (chief advisor to the emir) of Zazzau, one of the region's leading Islamic jurists, helped British authorities craft a 1954 memo providing legal justification for targeting NEPU members who spoke out publicly against the dominance of the masu sarauta with shari'ah prohibitions against slander and "insulting behavior." Not surprisingly, the NPC successfully used these advantages to win at the polls and prevent more substantial reforms.

The 1966 coup that ended Nigeria's first democratic experiment also triggered the secession of the country's

Eastern Region as the "Republic of Biafra" and a bloody civil war from 1967 to 1970. The first half-decade of independence had already deepened ethnic and religious tensions in Nigeria, and the war brought these tensions to a head. Postwar reconciliation efforts attempted to ensure that power and access to government revenues and resources (expanded greatly during the 1970s as a result of massive spikes in international oil prices) would be shared equally across ethnic and religious communities. Yet sectarian conflict worsened, fueled by the expansion of evangelical Christian and Salafi Islamic movements that brokered few opportunities for ecumenical compromise.

Older forms of dissent also flourished. The most important was the massive outbreak of violence that took place in Kano—the north's largest city—in December 1980. It was led by Mohammed Marwa, known locally as Maitatsine (He Who Curses), a native of northern Cameroon who had come to Nigeria in the early 1960s. Despite having been arrested, imprisoned, and even deported several times over the intervening decades, Marwa built up a sizeable local following. His teachings were esoteric and seen by many as blasphemous, driven by his belief that he was a prophet unto himself. Echoing Mallam Zum'atu in spirit (if not in the specifics), he taught the rejection of Western influence, technology, and education.

Marwa's message held special appeal to the almajirai, who had fallen on hard times. Historically, they had supported their studies by a combination of begging and labor in fields such as construction, market portering, and cloth dying. But as oil money flooded into Kano, traditional mud-brick construction was replaced by steel and concrete, porters by cars, and the dye pits by commercial textile mills. Meanwhile, many affluent locals came to regard the scruffy almajirai as eyesores. Marwa capitalized on these transformations, preaching loudly against the conspicuous consumption of Kano's elites.

Overtures from the state government to tone down Maitatsine's rhetoric failed, and, by the end of 1980, authorities were threatening to tear down his compound. On December 18, four highly armed police units were attacked by men wielding little more than homemade weaponry. The military was called in, an entire neighborhood razed, and more than four thousand declared dead. (Unofficial tallies put the number closer to ten thousand.) Marwa was killed in police custody, and an official inquiry praised the security forces' actions. Over the next five years, sect members staged at least a half-dozen uprisings, including several in territories later terrorized by Boko Haram. Each was put down by the full might of the military.

What lessons can we draw from this violent legacy? To be clear, armed struggle is hardly the only way northern Nigerian Muslims express their frustrations with the status quo. Signs of growing spiritual discontent are often subtle, embedded in quiet conversations or the sermons of dissident preachers such as Mohammed Yusuf. Even fashion choices (men's trousers that end high above the ankle align the wearer with the Salafi movement, turbans and hijabs with globalized notions of Islamic piety) can send signals. In Nigeria, mosques are a particularly important site for emerging dissent, since weak governmental supervision allows nearly anyone with the money and influence to obtain a plot of land to sponsor a new one. Meanwhile, fights over who controls older, more influential mosques have frequently bubbled over into testy confrontations and even violence, pitting members of centuries-old Sufi brotherhoods against the newer Salafi movements, Salafis against each other, and nearly everyone else against Nigeria's small and threatened Shi'a community.

During times of strain, these "quiet" conflicts can spark flames. Nigeria's religious riots often begin with some small grievance (accusations of a Christian market trader in a Muslim community defiling a Qur'an, confrontations between Muslim and Christian university organizations over access to a campus space) and evolve into mass violence over a few days. Then, the flames die down into embers, ready for re-ignition at the next provocation. But when the powers that be are faced with sustained criticism and organized dissent, the historical lesson is that, more often than not, they will summon the military force and political will to put down their opposition, even if the civilian cost is alarming.

In the long run, this is a high-risk strategy. Since the end of its civil war—a watershed moment in the Nigerian state's history of violence, with a million or more civilian casualties—these small flare-ups have become more common, driven by massive underlying shifts in the region's economic and social circumstances. Rapid urbanization, rising inequality, a dearth of meaningful employment opportunities for youth, and even the breakdown of older systems of social surveillance that allowed local authorities to keep a handle on the presence of "strangers" in tight-knit neighborhoods all help create an atmosphere of uncertainty and even fear in many Nigerian communities. These fears, and the violence they have justified, have laid much of the groundwork for Boko Haram's emergence.

Nigerian Salafism, a Short History

If a long history of state violence is one important piece of Boko Haram's origin story, it is fair to say that ideas and ideologies matter too. Even among those who seek a social revolution in the name of Islam, only a small subset ever justifies violence in the name of its faith. Still, the rise of Salafi theology across northern Nigeria since the 1950s and 1960s plays an important part in our story.

Earlier we defined Salafism as a movement to purify Muslim societies by adopting, as literally as possible, the beliefs and practices of the Prophet and his early community. More broadly, Salafism is a style of argument about religious truth and how we know it that emphasizes the importance of engaging directly with the "core" texts of Islamic revelation and a handful of influential theologians. It is also a claim to certainty. Salafi Muslims believe that by definition, theirs is the pure, authentic version of the faith and that they have the sources to prove it.

Intellectually, Salafism dates back to at least as early as the fourteenth-century Damascene theologian Ibn Taymiyya, who called for eliminating what he saw as the accumulated mistakes, errors, and heresies that had accumulated in Islamic theology in the generations following the Prophet's death. These concerns were revived by the Wahhabist movement, founded in the mid-eighteenth century by the Arabian cleric Muhammad ibn ʿAbd al-Wahhab. ʿAbd al-Wahhab's emphasis on the absolute Oneness of God (*tawhid*) and the dangers of bidʿa led him to declare that Muslims who failed to share his commitments were unbelievers. Still, most scholars agree that contemporary Salafism is a fundamentally twentieth-century movement, profoundly shaped by the massive social and intellectual upheavals of colonization and decolonization.

But while most Salafis are deeply conservative, they are hardly defenders of the status quo. Even as they look to the past for theological inspiration, what modern Salafism proposes is revolutionary, in the sense that achieving its goals requires rewriting the social order. Analyses that dismiss Mohammed Yusuf's rejection of

"Western" education and science or the barbaric violence of groups such as ISIS and Boko Haram as "medieval" tend to miss the point that the very idea of attempting to systematically engineer a utopian society—even if the inspiration is an ancient religious text—is decidedly modernist.

In Nigeria, Salafism's rise coincided with efforts by the British colonial government to invest in new institutions and opportunities for Islamic higher education. Under the policy of indirect rule, British authorities maintained a system of Islamic courts across northern Nigeria and required trained Muslim judges to staff them. In order to "improve" and standardize their educations, these authorities created a series of training colleges in the 1930s and 1940s designed to teach Islamic jurisprudence in a routinized, systematic way, emphasizing Arabic literacy, direct contact with canonical legal texts, and standardized syllabi and testing. They also created opportunities for study abroad in the Arab world, where young Nigerian scholars could be exposed to globalizing trends in Islamic theology and jurisprudence. Graduates of these programs became leaders in the growing movement to revitalize the role of Islam in public life following independence.

The most influential was Sheikh Abubakar Gumi. A graduate of Kano's British-founded School for Arabic Studies and recipient of a scholarship for advanced training in Sudan, Gumi had a state-funded religious education that prepared him for a career as a judge and educator, but he soon became known as a gadfly, quick to criticize local religious and political authorities. In 1955, he was named head of the Northern Nigerian delegation during the annual pilgrimage to Mecca, a position that brought him into contact with his future political patron, Sardauna Ahmadu Bello. With Bello's backing, he rose through the judicial ranks, eventually becoming the senior judge of the entire Northern Nigerian shari'ah court system. By the early 1970s, Gumi was arguably the most prominent Muslim intellectual in Nigeria, writing best-selling religious tracts that outlined an increasingly Salafi worldview and appearing regularly on national radio to offer *tafsir* (interpretation of holy texts).

In 1978, Gumi's followers founded Jama'atu Izalat al-Bid'ah wa Iqamat al Sunna (the Society for the Removal of Innovation and the Restoration of Tradition), or Izala for short. Izala attracted a broad following among the middle class, entrepreneurs, women, and youth. A substantial part of its appeal was its condemnation of "traditional" celebrations such as weddings, the costs of which often exceeded the income of all but the wealthiest members of society. Another was its promotion of women's education, which it saw as a key to expanding piety. Adopting a politically "activist" orientation, Izala also positioned itself as arguably the leading voice for Muslim interests in Nigeria.

Izala's monopoly on Salafi discourse in Nigeria was short-lived. By the mid-1980s, the organization had split around leadership, finances, and doctrine, pitting one faction based in the city of Jos against another in the former Northern region capital of Kaduna. These divisions were amplified by a generational fissure, as a new cohort of Salafi intellectuals returned from educational institutions abroad, particularly the Islamic University of Medina (IUM). Members of this informal network, many of whom eventually settled in Kano, were less committed to anti-Sufism and more to the notion of promoting Salafism independent of any particular movement or institution. Eventually, they took on the name Ahlussunnah (Ahl al-Sunna, or "people of the Prophet's teachings"), while their members moved into key leadership positions in state-based religious institutions and mosques.

By the late 1990s, Ahlussunnah's most visible face was an IUM graduate named Ja'afar Mahmoud Adam, a charismatic scholar whose media savvy made him a natural successor to Gumi's popularity. Adam was a highly sought-after preacher, and videos of his tafsir remain hot sellers. He was also a reluctant but effective political advocate, serving as a member of the committee to review Kano State's draft shari'ah legal code in the early 2000s and advocating for Salafis to participate in politics lest the country's new democracy fail to represent Muslim interests. Adam's involvement in political affairs was less overt than that of Gumi, who often engaged in explicitly partisan activism. Yet he and other like-minded Salafis were important electoral players in the 2007 Kano State elections, throwing their weight against the incumbent governor, Ibrahim Shekarau, whom they accused using a public campaign for shari'ah for his own aggrandizement.

Members of Ahlussunnah—and Adam in particular—also built reputations as skillful theological debaters. Ahlussunnah preachers eagerly engaged in public arguments (often filmed and distributed on video CDs and DVDs) with opponents and critics and were highly sought-after as guest lecturers. Adam was invited to preach numerous times in a private mosque sponsored by a prominent Salafi-aligned businessman in Maiduguri named Alhaji Mohammed Ndimi. It was here that he likely first encountered Mohammed Yusuf—often described as his "student," although the full scope of their relationship is not entirely clear. In the last years of his life, Adam's most famous public lectures were biting criticisms of Yusuf, who had become well-known for using Salafi theology to reject all engagement with Nigeria's democratic government and its institutions. Adam was assassinated in April 2007 by attackers still unknown but now widely thought to be Yusuf's followers.

The Nigerian Salafi community has long grappled with its relationship with violence. Historically, Nigerian Salafis have rejected calls for violent jihad, even as they have frequently invoked the Shehu's legacy and occasionally offered tacit support for projihadist rhetoric following the US invasions of Iraq and Afghanistan. Yet

rumors and unevenly sourced reports have also suggested that by the late 1990s or early 2000s, supporters
of Salafi-jihadist ideology were circulating within the
underbelly of the Nigerian Salafi community, linking
locals with the rhetoric (and perhaps the resources)
of global jihadist networks. Whatever the case, Mohammed Yusuf's rise to prominence as a popular,
charismatic voice for jihad in Nigeria helped bring
these questions to the forefront.

2

The Evolution of a Movement

Who Was Mohammed Yusuf?

For such an important figure, our knowledge of Mohammed Yusuf's life is remarkably sketchy. Biographical
information, especially about his youth and early career,
is limited. And since a surprisingly large amount of what
we do know comes from his opponents, it is hard to
separate the truth from accusations made to discredit
him. Many of the most common claims about Yusuf's
journey from small-time cleric to leading extremist can
be traced to just a handful of original sources of uncertain reliability, and there are some things we will never
know.

Most agree that Yusuf was born in 1970 in Girgir,
a small village in western Yobe State. Religious dissent
was the family business. His father was a small-time
cleric with a reputation for challenging local religious
authorities, and at least one leading Boko Haram critic,
a Salafi preacher named Sheikh Muhammad Auwal Al-
bani Zaria, has alleged that his death in 1980 was part
of the Maitatisine uprising in Kano. After his father

died, Yusuf came under the care of a family friend, the Maiduguri-based businessman named Alhaji Baba Fugu Mohammed. Fugu saw to his young ward's Qur'anic education, although he seems not to have pressed him to attend state-run schools or even (reputedly) to learn to speak English fluently.

By the early 1990s, Yusuf had become a *mallam* in his own right, preaching in the town of Potiskum. Around 1995, he joined a local Salafi group in Maiduguri founded by a cleric named Abubakar Lawan. When Lawan left to study at IUM, Yusuf took over as one of the group's leaders. By 2000, he was a popular religious figure in Maiduguri, appearing regularly at the Ndimi Mosque in the company of a group of young Salafis— including students at the University of Maiduguri (UNIMAID, as it is known locally)—who had grown disenchanted with Nigerian society and politics.

Over the next few years, Yusuf was a star on the rise. He came to the attention of the Ahlussunnah network and seems to have served for a time as Sheikh Ja'afar Adam's local representative. Along the way, his message evolved in more confrontational directions. As British journalist Andrew Walker has documented, UNIMAID in those days was an institution in flux. These were the waning years of the Sani Abacha dictatorship, and Nigeria was an international pariah. The children of elites found it difficult to gain admission to prestigious international universities, and UNIMAID saw an uptick in wealthy and well-connected students. This influx had a profound impact on campus culture, which many "ordinary" students saw as dominated by ostentatious displays of wealth and booze, dancing, and gambling. Just as with the barracks of the colonial era, locals perceived UNIMAID as a space where elites and cultural outsiders could flout the norms of Muslim society, free from consequence.[1] Some of the most critical students were drawn to Salafi activism, which offered a ready-made story about the relationship between elite corruption and moral decay.

Encouraged by these new connections, Yusuf's preaching took on a newly combative tone toward "Western" educational influence and Nigeria's new civilian government. Sometime in 2001 or 2002, he left (or was barred from) the Ndimi Mosque, taking with him a small but growing collection of followers, including future "Taliban" stalwart Aminu "Tashen-Ilimi" (a pseudonym that translates roughly to "Growing Knowledge"). Their new mosque, named for Ibn Taymiyya, occupied a plot of land leased by Baba Fugu Mohammed in the "low-cost" Anguwan Doki neighborhood. It would remain there until 2009, when it was destroyed in the confrontation that cost Yusuf his life.

The Shari'ah Revolution

Another important piece to Yusuf's rise was the shari'ah controversy that was dominating the Nigerian headlines in those days. Beginning in the mid-1990s, a trend of political liberalization across the Muslim world revealed something unexpected: broad popular support for both democracy *and* Islamic law. As surveys showed, large majorities of Muslims embrace both democracy as the best form of government and a desire to recognize Islamic values in law. In countries as different as Indonesia (where local governments have passed hundreds of shari'ah-inspired laws since 1998) and Nigeria, politicians and ordinary citizens alike have responded to the new opportunities posed by democratic politics by attempting to make shari'ah and democracy work together.

"Restoring" shari'ah to its former glories is rarely a simple proposition, however. In Nigeria, Muslims lost a debate in the late 1970s over whether or not the federal government should create a national shari'ah court of appeals for family and civil law cases (which have never stopped being tried under shari'ah in many communities across northern Nigeria), and few political leaders had seriously considered reviving the conflict. Indeed, in 1999, the entire idea seems to have been floated as a temporary ploy by Zamfara State politicians looking to burnish their religious credentials during a tough election campaign. But after the first pro-shari'ah rallies, massive popular support had other states paying close attention. In a few, local governors and legislatures enthusiastically embraced shari'ah, rushing to put together legal codes and enact new social policies. In others, politicians were more reluctant, fearing that they might lose control over this new populist wave.

One of the most reluctant was Borno's governor, Mala Kachalla, whose administration dragged its feet for over three years: appointing a committee to "study" the issue in January 2000, "launching" shari'ah to the public in August 2000, and compiling and enacting the necessary legal code to administer it in March 2003. For his efforts, Kachalla was replaced on his party's ticket for the 2003 gubernatorial election by Ali Modu Sheriff, a federal senator and one of the leading financiers behind Kachalla's 1999 campaign. Kachalla chose to contest the election under a new party banner, and the campaign turned dirty.

Sheriff recognized that Kachalla's reluctance offered a political opening, and his efforts to find allies within the local religious leadership led him to Yusuf's congregation. In exchange for Yusuf's support from the pulpit and on the street (a 2011 government report found that Sheriff had organized a political militia that recruited future Boko Haram members to terrorize Kachalla supporters), his community would receive a range of financial benefits, including cash, a fleet of motorcycles, and the candidate's commitment to advancing "real" shari'ah. In the rough-and-tumble world of Nigerian politics, these sorts of arrangements are not rare. But the Sheriff/Yusuf bargain went a step further. Following his victory, Sheriff appointed as state commissioner of religious affairs a man named Buji Foi, allegedly a key financier of Yusuf's expanding operations. Like Yusuf, Foi eventually fell out of favor with Sheriff, and he was killed by state security agents while in custody during the July 2009 uprising.

It is not clear how important Yusuf's support was to Sheriff's election victory. But in late 2002 or early 2003, their relationship became a source of tension within Yusuf's congregation, particularly among those who had influenced his break with the Ndimi Mosque. Some sources have counted among these hard-liners the future Boko Haram leader Abubakar Shekau, whose involvement with the Hijra Group has been frequently suggested but never conclusively proven. Although specifics remain frustratingly vague, Yusuf's support for Sheriff likely played a role in the intragroup tensions that led to the events at Kanama.

Yusuf eventually saw for himself that Sheriff had few concrete plans for expanding shari'ah or working more closely with the Salafi community. Following a few frustrating efforts to participate in the state's official shari'ah-implementation planning process, Yusuf cut things off with Sheriff, although not without retaining the financial fruits of the original arrangement. Some of the motorcycles they received were photographed amid the rubble of Yusuf's mosque after the 2009 uprising, having seen a half-decade of use as motorcycle taxis (*achaba,* in the local parlance), providing work to the movement's unemployed young men.

When the dust settled after Kanama, Yusuf found himself the target of police suspicion. Although he had left Maiduguri for Saudi Arabia sometime in late 2003 or early 2004, the lead Nigerian police investigator on the Hijra Group case publicly named him as one of the group's masterminds and announced that he was working with Interpol to arrest him. In this light, his convenient departure seems more like a coordinated effort to escape arrest. This was confirmed by a 2009 interview with then Borno deputy governor Adamu Dibal, who claimed to have met with Yusuf in 2004 in Saudi Arabia. As Dibal tells it, Yusuf came to him seeking assistance to return home, insisting that he had played no role in the Yobe attacks. Through his connections with Nigerian national intelligence, Dibal facilitated a reconciliation, and Yusuf was allowed to come back to Maiduguri.[2]

The Yusufiyya

The community to which Yusuf returned was in a state of flux. It was already the target of police attention, and Yusuf's rhetoric from the pulpit and in audio recordings was downright incendiary. Relations with the "mainstream" Salafi community, including Yusuf's erstwhile mentor Sheikh Ja'afar Adam and the Ahlussunnah network, were also souring. Privately, Adam and his allies had begun pressuring Yusuf in the hope of moderating some of his more extreme positions, including his now-strict prohibition of Western-style education and of employment in government. By 2004, Adam was airing the conflict in public, hoping to use popular opinion to dissuade Yusuf from what he saw as his excesses.

As former Agence France-Press (AFP) reporter Mike Smith notes, Yusuf's personal charisma and knack for speaking about the problems facing ordinary Nigerians held an undeniable appeal. One of Smith's interviewees, a Lagos-born Christian named Anayo Adibe, noted that "because his preachings were usually against the ruling class," his message held a special resonance with those who suffered from the region's poverty or daily encounters with official corruption. Adibe, who occasionally crossed paths with Yusuf in his role as family lawyer for Yusuf's father-in-law, Baba Fugu Mohammed, said that even though he rejected the movement's eventual violence, on issues such as Yusuf's views on government he "agreed with him—completely."[3]

Yusuf was also an effective community builder. He encouraged his supporters to contribute their own resources to the cause and established business opportunities for unemployed members. Sales of audio and video recordings of his sermons were another source of revenue. It is also likely that some funds came in the form of private donations from wealthy benefactors. Buji Foi was one probable source (although Sheriff has repeatedly denied that Foi used government funds, either with his knowledge or without), but there were almost certainly a few others. And, of course, there are the reports of cash from al-Qaeda, Al Mutada, and other international sources, although there is little direct evidence that the money was received or what it was used for.

How popular was Yusuf's movement, exactly? One popular but unsubstantiated claim, which originated with an obscure 2009 Nigerian academic paper but has been frequently repeated, suggested that Yusuf had nearly three hundred thousand eager supporters across Chad, Niger, and northern Nigeria.[4] This depiction contrasts with local sources, which tell the story of a smaller, more tightly knit group united by its religious convictions in pursuit of a space—physical and symbolic—apart from the Nigerian state. In a 2006 interview, Yusuf described his flock as "3,000 students," all committed to the creation of an "Islamic system of governance."[5] His influence went beyond that core group, of course—its outreach spanned into nearby states such as Yobe and Bauchi, and journalists have found family members from across the region who claim their loved ones were drawn into the group's orbit from afar. Yusuf's followers were also more economically diverse than simplistic accounts suggest and included not only the downtrodden but also members of the region's upper class and a host of traders and businessmen who saw the organization as a source of financial *and* spiritual opportunity.

One important observer during these years was the journalist Ahmed Salkida. Salkida was a well-known member of the Maiduguri press corps who frequently sparred with the Sheriff administration over the gap between its promises and performance. And as a convert to Islam who had watched the growth of the Yusufiyya movement firsthand, he spent time with many of the group's key figures, attending preaching sessions in his off-hours and developing what he has described as a familiar, even friendly relationship with Yusuf himself. Yusuf reciprocated by taking a personal interest in Salkida and his family. Salkida has said that he was even offered a job by Yusuf as the publisher and editor of a newspaper for the group, He responded to the invitation by insisting on total editorial control and the publication of a regular column featuring viewpoints that challenged Yusuf's orthodoxy. Not surprisingly, the job never materialized.

Salkida's reporting offers a unique account of how the Yusufiyya built its community. As he tells it, Yusuf's genius was his ability to reach an audience of youth who, despite the promise of the 1999 democratic transition, continued to feel as though they had no voice in their own society. Although his radical reputation prevented him from preaching in the region's biggest mosques or gaining airtime on local television and radio, his outreach efforts targeted unemployed recent graduates and current students, many of whom had looked to their schools as paths toward upward mobility and had instead found little more than "incessant strikes, cult activities, [and] widespread malpractices."[6]

Drawn in by the message, these young people found an organization that offered jobs and the prospect of leadership positions but also a sense of dignity and self-worth. By the late 2000s, the Yusufiyya was a "state within a state," capable of providing for the care and livelihoods of hundreds of followers. For governance, it possessed "a cabinet, the Shura [governing "consultative" council], the Hisbah [a religious police force], the brigade of guards, [and] a military wing," while economically it could boast "a large farm [and] an effective microfinance scheme."[7] Although Yusuf himself was arrested no fewer than three times from 2006 to 2007, his broader activities seem to have gone largely unchallenged by the authorities.

Is "Boko" *Haram?*

There has been a lot of confusion about Boko Haram's religious ideology and its role in the group's transformation into a jihadist insurgency. Most writing about it has focused, understandably but often uncritically, on Yusuf's condemnation of "Western" education and science as a stand-alone ideology, one that fits into established narratives about a radical Islamic "war on girls" and their access to education. But this reading of what Yusuf and his movement stood for—and what Boko Haram stands for today—is incomplete.

Part of the confusion stems from taking Yusuf's many proclamations, which ranged from declaring that being a sports fan was *haram* ("forbidden," because it might cause Muslims to admire non-Muslims) to arguing that it was God (and not the evaporation cycle) that caused rain, out of context in a way that highlights their oddness to Western ears rather than their theological underpinnings. Another stems from the first academic analyses of the group, which were quick to describe Yusuf's movement in terms of the Maitatsine crisis of three decades earlier. On the surface, the similarities were obvious. Both were populist, insular, led by charismatic ideologues, and clashed repeatedly with local authorities. But beneath, they were profoundly different. Yusuf's teachings on boko were not, as were Maitatsine's, free-floating claims based in little more than his own esoteric beliefs. Yusuf was a self-conscious and intentional participant in the Nigerian (and, indeed, the global) Salafi Muslim community, and his preaching—about education, science, government, and the rest—was part of a broader debate about who could "speak" for the community in the public sphere and about what its role should be in political affairs.

What exactly did Yusuf believe, and why did it generate so much conflict? As the American scholar Alex Thurston has argued, at their core Yusuf's teachings were about defending the purity and exclusivity of the Muslim community. He was, in this sense, not only a Salafi but also what scholars have come to call a "Salafi-jihadi." Salafi-jihadis play up arguments that justify rejecting and even engaging in violence against "non-Islamic" governments and that describe believers as a "Muslim vanguard beset by hostile authorities and surrounded by hypocrites and enemies." In his 2009 manifesto *Hādhihi ʿAqīdatunā wa-Manhaj Daʿwatinā* (This is our creed and the method of our preaching),

Yusuf drew heavily on a concept borrowed from Middle Eastern Salafi-jihadi thinkers called "*al-wala' wa-l-bara*" (loyalty and disavowal). This idea was originally applied by nineteenth-century Arabian thinkers to prohibit tribal and religious leaders from seeking the assistance of non-Muslims. But in the modern context, it is often interpreted to mean that Muslims have an obligation to challenge non-Muslim rulers and the things they stand for. Yusuf taught that Muslims must "make a complete disavowal of every form of unbelief," setting them apart from not only their neighbors but also from the entirety of the secular Nigerian state.[8] Boko, understood broadly as anything from Western, scientific accounts of the universe's origins to constitutional government, fits precisely this bill.

Yusuf's opponents, including Sheikh Ja'afar Adam, attacked these arguments on a number of grounds. The first was the question of Yusuf's authority. For them, Yusuf's rapid rise to prominence belied the thinness of his education. Whereas members of the Ahlussunnah network could point to their university degrees and their extensive knowledge of the Salafi intellectual canon, they saw Yusuf as unsophisticated and parochial. As Adam put it, "What do you [Yusuf] know about the history of various struggles for Islam? How many years did al-Banna [the founder of the Egyptian Muslim Brotherhood] spend in struggle? . . . What about the national liberation struggle in Algeria where one million martyrs were lost to the French colonizers? . . . Nearer to home how many battles did Usman dan Fodio fight? Apart from dan Fodio's name, what do you know about his battles?"[9]

Yusuf's intellectual shortcuts were not the only concern. Although many anti-Yusuf Salafis had mixed feelings about political participation, most believed they had a responsibility to both criticize and, when possible, influence the government's actions. Yusuf's blanket condemnations of Muslims' participation in public affairs did little, to their minds, to address the practical needs of Muslims and much to ensure their marginalization.

The battle between Yusuf and Adam over the soul of Nigerian Salafism reached its crescendo in April 2007 when Adam was brutally murdered in his mosque by still-unknown gunmen. Initially, suspicion fell on the Shekarau administration in Kano, which Adam had opposed in an election campaign that ended the day after the assassination. But over the course of several years, the focus shifted to Yusuf and his supporters, to the point where most sources now simply state Boko Haram's involvement as a matter of fact. The truth is that we may never know who murdered Adam. But Boko Haram's later assassinations of Muslim clerics who preached against it casts an air of plausibility on the story of its involvement.

Many Salafi clerics have worked hard since 2009 to maintain an ideological bulwark against Boko Haram's appeal. Following Adam's initial playbook, they focus on denying radical antistate voices the space to spread their message, by controlling access to mosques, the media, and other outlets. Some, like Ahmed Gumi, the son of former Izala leader Abubakar Gumi, even go so far as to offer a hesitant endorsement of Western governmental models (including democracy) so long as they offer tangible benefits to Muslim communities such as security and accountability. But Nigerian Salafis face hard challenges in their efforts to prevent the "next Yusuf." Criticize government too loudly—risk being tarred with the Boko Haram brush. Collaborate too readily—lose their popular support. This fine line complicates efforts to distill a popular theological response to Boko Haram.[10]

How was Yusuf seen outside Salafi circles? Most of the broader Islamic establishment regarded him and his followers as poorly educated rabble-rousers. And as Salkida wrote in March 2009, many ordinary citizens "wished that Mohammed Yusuf would never get another chance to see the light of day or, if he did, he would be banished to somewhere far away." Yusuf's success in attracting youth members to abandon school alienated parents, religious authorities, and community leaders, many of whom saw him as a self-interested charlatan. As one student put it, "Malam Yusuf has never provided an alternative means by which Muslims could contribute to the global intellectual exercise, let alone [how] they could learn to improve their wellbeing. Instead, he has advocated a total boycott."[11] It was this tension between

the "total boycott" mentality and the flexibility necessary to survive in the face of a Nigerian state prone to
lashing out at anything it could not control that proved
Yusuf's undoing.

Showdown in Maiduguri

By 2007, Yusuf's activities finally began to draw a serious
governmental response. This was motivated at least in
part by a growing national unease about the prospects
for extremist violence across the north. A series of attacks
on government offices near Kano in April 2007—just
days after Adam's assassination—were widely attributed
to the remnants of the old "Nigerian Taliban," which
had resurfaced a year earlier when Aminu Tashen-Ilimi
gave an interview to AFP reporters threatening a violent
"comeback." A few months earlier, Bello Iliya Damagun,
the director of the *Daily Trust*, one of Nigeria's largest
newspapers, was arrested on allegations that he had
worked with members of the Nigerian Taliban to acquire
funds from an al-Qaeda affiliate. Damagun was detained
(but never charged) in 2004 for allegedly helping send
young Nigerians to Mauritania for training in an AQIM
camp, and his case drew national attention as one of the
first potential public links between Nigerian jihadists
and al-Qaeda. Damagun insisted on his innocence, and
all charges against him were dropped in 2009. However,
a wave of arrests that followed over the next year, including a half-dozen Nigerians with alleged connections to
Algerian jihadist groups, helped raise fears that Yusuf

might be involved in something more dangerous than microfinance and farming.

In November 2008, Yusuf was taken into custody by the notorious State Security Service (SSS) on charges of "public incitement to violence." After his arrest, Yusuf was moved to Abuja, where he was held until a January 2009 hearing. Despite a reading of charges that included attempted infiltration of the police and the SSS in order to gather arms and launch "a full-fledged religious war," he was granted bail (N250,000, roughly $1,600) and released. In April, the case was dismissed, following the apparent failure of the SSS to produce adequate evidence.

By the time he returned, another long-simmering conflict was boiling over. In 2007, Governor Sheriff sought and won a second term as governor. This time, his agenda had little to do with shari'ah, focusing instead on the usual combination of populist economic development policies and law-and-order language most Nigerian politicians tend to fall back on. One of his key proposals was the creation of a new joint police-military task force code-named "Operation Flush," designed to address growing crime and lawlessness throughout Maiduguri.

On its face, Operation Flush served an important need. Residents had reported a growing threat from petty theft and outright highway robbery, while the police seemed at best overwhelmed and at worst incompetent. Similarly, Borno State had become an epicenter for devastating motor vehicle accidents, overwhelming the efforts of traffic authorities and local hospitals. The victims were often commercial motorcyclists and their passengers, an increasingly common sight on Nigerian roads beginning in the 1980s and 1990s. In cities such as Maiduguri, where public transportation infrastructure had seen little investment for decades, achaba were ubiquitous. Often, the bikes were gifts (such as Sheriff's "donation" to the Yusufiyya in 2003) from community leaders and politicians, who viewed them as a cheap investment in an important political demographic.

Many well-off Nigerians consider achaba a public nuisance. Cheap, underpowered, and imported from China, the bikes are loud and belch fumes, and the riders are notorious for navigating traffic without regard for automobiles or each other. And at their worst, achaba drivers are known for beating and even killing car operators who injure their comrades. There have been numerous efforts led by wealthy urbanites and their supporters in state government to ban them in Lagos, Abuja, Kano, and elsewhere, efforts that became more successful with the importation of motorized tricycles (the famous "*keke NAPEP*," named after the National Poverty Eradication Programme that helped distribute them) in the mid-2000s. In late 2008, the federal Nigerian Police Force began enforcing a new law that all motorcyclists and their passengers must henceforth wear safety helmets at all times.

This initiative was bound to fail. Helmets are expensive, and many could not afford them. Achaba riders knew that the brunt of the enforcement would come in the form of roadblocks where police would harass and abuse them with beatings or the notorious "frog jump," where the unfortunate victims are forced (often at gunpoint) to hop up and down from a squatting position until they collapse. Their only choice would be bribes or creative alternatives such as the hollowed-out calabashes riders in Kano reportedly wore to fool the police.

Nor were achaba drivers Operation Flush's only victims. Within months, persistent rumors of illegal arrests, lengthy detentions without formal charges, and brutality against civilians, including extrajudicial killings, began to circulate around Borno State. Other reports pointed to widespread accusations that the unit used its newfound power to engage in extortion and other forms of corruption. Foreshadowing not only the July crackdown but also the ensuing violence, Salkida suggested that for many victims of Operation Flush's excesses, radical antigovernment sentiments had begun to offer an attractive alternative to acquiescence.

For Yusuf, Operation Flush was the last straw. The task force had a particular mandate for reining in the Yusufiyya, which Sheriff (rightly, in retrospect) now regarded as a major threat to public order. In response, Yusuf's shura council issued a press release in February outlining its position of "non-violen[t] . . . non-cooperation towards the government." The second paragraph, however, is worth quoting in its entirety:

It should, nevertheless, be noted that our stand should not be interpreted or misrepresented to mean a negation of the Islamic concept of Jihaad [*sic*] which we always believe to be valid upon the attainment of three basic prerequisites: an Islamic leader, state and flag which are largely not obtainable in the current Nigerian setting. However, we believe that Jihaad [*sic*] for the defense of Islam and Muslims when attacked at anytime is always valid and does not require the mentioned prerequisites.[12]

Around Borno, rumors that the Yusufiyya was stockpiling weapons became louder, supported by allegations that emerged after the uprising that Yusuf had sent several members to Afghanistan to learn bomb-making. The real breaking point, however, came on June 11, 2009, when members of the Yusufiyya staged a funeral procession for four of their fellows who had died in a traffic accident the day before. Along its route, the procession was stopped by Operation Flush agents, who targeted the group's achaba riders for special attention.

The Yusufiyya interpreted this particular traffic stop as a provocation and formed a threatening crowd around the officers. The police fired, and seventeen group members were wounded or killed. The next day—a Friday, as luck would have it, which is when Muslims congregate for prayer—Yusuf's sermon (later described as an "open letter" to the Nigerian government) offered a laundry list of the abuses his community had suffered, including threats against group members who had gone to the hospital to donate blood after the attack. His discussion of police conduct set the stage for what was to come:

> In Islam when we have a truce with someone not to harm, and he turns his back against our agreement, God has stated "Once they turn their back on their promises after the agreement and they accuse your religion, fight them for they don't keep their promises, perhaps war will stop them." Their utterances are common, you will hear them say: "I am a soldier," "I am not a politician," and "we don't negotiate with people," Alas! It is all falsehood unless if they have not been oppressed.
>
> And we thank Allah that our members have stood their ground on that day without fear. Our ability to stand their oppression was a special gift from Allah who removed fear out of the minds of the believers. This is something to celebrate by thanking God. We give Glory to Allah for our ability to withstand oppression despite the variety of weapons they carried and the pool of blood we saw, yet we did not retreat. This is not the matter of saying that it was Allah who destined that such will happen! Yes, Allah has destined that right from the beginning, just like the way he destined a thief to steal and face amputation, and the way he destined a drunkard who drinks and get lashed eighty times. I hope it is well understood.

> Therefore the blood of a believer cannot be shed
> by an unbeliever in his own land . . . How can you
> attack people who were on their way for a burial?
> What you should have done was to announce a
> specific date where we will encounter each other![13]

Over the next month, there were repeated warnings that Yusuf and his followers were preparing for exactly such a "specific date." Sympathizers converged on the Ibn Taymiyya Mosque, while others staged preparations elsewhere. Sometime during the week of July 19, nine members were arrested in Biu (another city in Borno), allegedly carrying bombs. Two were taken into custody near Yusuf's Bauchi State farm, and a third blew himself up in a failed bomb-making attempt.

The uprising began on July 26, 2009, as hundreds of members staged an early-morning attack on a police station in Bauchi. One hundred and fifty were reported killed. Shortly afterward, Yusuf gave Salkida a final phone interview, threatening that "his men were ready to die to ensure the institution of a strict Islamic society."[14] On the 27th, a series of coordinated assaults on the Maiduguri police headquarters, a local prison, and other government targets left about ninety members of the Yusufiyya and a handful of police dead, with further outbreaks in Yobe and Kano States. The next day, government forces mounted their response, a timing influenced by President Umaru Musa Yar'Adua's impending departure to Brazil. Reinforcements from Lagos and elsewhere staged a full-out assault on the group's base of operations, while engaging in bloody confrontations throughout Maiduguri. The battle continued on the 29th, with Yusuf temporarily evading capture as his home and mosque were destroyed. In all, roughly eight hundred died, the vast majority of them Yusuf's followers.

On July 30, just as the violence was dying down, Yusuf was apprehended. In the only official photo of him in custody, he is shirtless, has a bandaged left arm, and is surrounded by security agents in battle gear. At some point, he was handed over to the police, who conducted a brief interrogation. Video smuggled out and posted to YouTube showed him in handcuffs, calmly responding to questions. His interrogators zeroed in on the contradictions between his public ideology and what they had found at his compound, asking pointed questions about technology ("At your place we found computers. . . . Are all that [*sic*] not products of [Western] knowledge?") and his lifestyle ("How come you are eating good food, . . . you are driving good cars, and wearing good clothes while you are forcing your followers to sell their belongings and live mostly on dates and water?"). Yusuf is remarkably candid for a man who must know he is unlikely to survive the day. One moment, he is debating theology ("Q: But Allah said in the Qur'an 'read,' that people should seek knowledge. . . . A: That's correct, but not the knowledge that contravenes the teachings of Islam."), the next deflecting any blame for the deaths of his followers back onto his captors ("Q: Now you have made us kill people that are innocent. What do you have to say? A: You bear responsibility on all those you killed.").[15]

The authorities initially claimed that Yusuf had been killed while trying to escape. What now seems clear is that at some point after his interrogation, Yusuf was simply taken outside the police station and shot. A picture of his corpse soon circulated among journalists—proof that he was dead and that the conflict was now over. Nigerian authorities declared victory on July 31, with a police spokesperson telling reporters that "the leader who they thought was invincible and immortal has now proved otherwise" and that "life [was] back to normal" across the region.[16]

The Aftermath

What might have become of Boko Haram if Yusuf had not been murdered or if Operation Flush had never targeted the Yusufiyya? Did his radical ideology and popularity make the group's transformation into a jihadist force inevitable? Or might some other religious authority have succeeded where Adam failed, bringing Yusuf back into the "mainstream" of Nigerian Salafism? Sadly, we'll never know.

What we do know is that for years Nigerian authorities failed to recognize how serious a threat Yusuf's movement posed. For Governor Sheriff and members of the political elite, it seemed unthinkable that a small group of rabble-rousers, however well organized and committed to their cause, could seriously disrupt the status quo. For the military and police, their blindness to the role of the violence they perpetrated in helping Yusuf's movement come together prevented them from recognizing that there would be no easy security solution once Boko Haram struck back. And the religious establishment—the imams, religious scholars, and traditional leaders—failed to recognize their own disconnect from the grassroots, trusting in their top-down criticism of Yusuf and his associates to dissuade ordinary Muslims from sympathizing with them while failing to grapple with their own role in the shari'ah-implementation project that had done little to solve real-life problems in local communities. These failures, and the continued inability of the most powerful members of Nigerian society to understand them, remain with us today.

Soon after Yusuf's murder, the remaining members of the Yusufiyya went underground. By most accounts, the Nigerian security services believed they had accomplished what they had hoped to with Maitatsine—a decapitation that also killed the body. If anything, the most common topic of discussion was the abuses by security forces, a persistent theme during the years to come. The day after Yusuf's murder, Minister of Information Dora Akunyili declared that while the government did not condone the police's actions, Yusuf's death was a good thing inasmuch as it had prevented further violence. Meanwhile, human rights activists called loudly for an investigation into Yusuf's death and the underlying causes of the violence, about which little accurate information had yet circulated. President Yar'Adua announced a full probe of the events leading up to the uprising, including allegations of police abuses and that the security services had failed to heed repeated warnings from religious leaders about Yusuf's movement.

Among the loudest critics were the family of Baba Fugu Mohammed, Yusuf's mentor and father-in-law. By most accounts, Fugu had little to do with the group's activities beyond his ownership of the land where their mosque was build. Nonetheless, the day after Yusuf's apprehension, he was "summoned" to appear before the police to answer questions. He appears to have gone willingly to his fate, presenting himself at the central police station in Maiduguri. The next day, his body appeared at the local morgue with a gunshot wound to the head.

Fugu's children insisted that not only had he played no part in the Yusufiyya's transformation into Boko Haram but that members of the family had attempted to warn local authorities about the group's potential for violence. In February 2010, they filed a wrongful death suit, naming Yar'Adua, Sheriff, and a host of high officials as plaintiffs. They also alleged that Fugu's properties had been illegally seized or destroyed, effectively leaving the family homeless. A court ruled in their favor and demanded the family receive an apology and a N100 million settlement (about $625,000 at the time), a sum that was finally paid out in 2012 after years of appeals. Sadly, Fugu's eldest son, Babakura, did not live to see it. He was assassinated (most likely by Boko Haram members) in September 2011, only days after meeting with former president Olusegun Obasanjo about assisting with negotiations to end the renewed conflict.

The New Boko Haram

During his interrogation, Mohammed Yusuf was asked if he had a second-in-command. The name he provided, Abubakar Shekau, was already well known to local authorities. Ironically, given that he has now been in the public eye significantly longer than Yusuf, we know even less about Shekau's biography than Yusuf's. Most sources peg him as roughly the same age as Yusuf and suggest he is originally from the area of Shekau village in central Yobe State. From his videos, it is apparent he speaks rudimentary English, suggesting that he has had

Figure 1. Abubakar Shekau, from a 2017 video released by his group

little Western-style education. Salkida reported meeting Shekau in 2005 or 2006, describing him as "devoted and modest," content to wear cheap clothes and ride an ordinary motorcycle.[17]

It is also clear that from the moment that Shekau took control of Yusuf's movement, he had broader and more deadly ambitions. Evidence recovered from the compound where Osama bin Laden was killed in Pakistan suggest that Shekau had begun to reach out to other global jihadist leaders within months (if not weeks) of the failed 2009 uprising in an effort to consolidate his own power and rebuild Yusuf's movement. Using connections to a handful of Nigerian former AQIM fighters who had participated in the uprising, Shekau was able to make indirect contact with AQIM's emir, Abd al-Malik Droukdel. Although Droukdel evidently authorized the transfer of €200,000 to Shekau's forces, there is little direct information about how these promises of support translated into action in Nigeria. It is likely that Shekau received at least some help in getting his rebuilt group off the ground in 2010 and 2011, but Shekau's penchant for violence and desire for total control would soon put him at odds with most of his potential external benefactors.

His first moment in the national limelight would come in July 2010. Several months before, Shekau—who had been wounded during the uprising—had arranged for an interview with a local journalist in Maiduguri. In it, he appears with a stack of religious texts and an

AK-47 as his backdrop. He claimed (inaccurately) that his group had only resorted to violence in self-defense and that the resulting bloodshed was entirely the government's fault. He also declared that he had taken over leadership of Yusuf's remaining followers, threatening retaliation against those who had killed his comrades. Most ominously, when asked whether or not it was inconsistent for a group so opposed to Western science and technology to use guns, Shekau replied that "God said we should get them [weapons], the Holy Prophet said we should get them."[18]

Retaliation came on September 7, with an assault on the federal prison in Bauchi. The attack was timed to coincide with the end of the evening prayer, just as the Muslim guards were preparing to break their Ramadan fast. Government sources reported five deaths during the fight but also admitted that a remarkable 721 prisoners (out of a total of 759) had escaped during the chaos, including 105 alleged Boko Haram members. Given that the prison is near the center of town—only a stone's throw from the central mosque—this was an audacious introduction to Boko Haram's new capabilities.

During the raid, the attackers dropped copies of two leaflets outside the prison. The first and shorter one was a calling card of sorts, explaining that the group's official name was not, in fact, Boko Haram but rather Jama'atu Alhlissunnah lidda' awati wal Jihad (roughly, "Salafis Committed to Spreading the Prophet's Message and Jihad"). The second pamphlet was part manifesto, part call to arms. It called out the group's solidarity with Muslims in Nigeria who faced violence from the government or their Christian neighbors and pointed out its fundamental peacefulness in the months and years before the July 2009 clash: "Everyone can attest to the fact that since we started our activities . . . we have never molested anyone. We only preached that it was forbidden to follow any path contrary to what Allah, through his Messenger—the Prophet Mohammed—commanded to follow."[19]

It was also a declaration of war. Henceforth, the pamphlet stated, "fighting this government is mandatory," and it called for "whoever can, [to] join" the group. Those that refused would be "accountable to Allah," left only to "watch what will happen." Ominously, it threatened harsh punishments for those who might inform to government officials on their activities, blaming these critics for the litany of abuses it had suffered the year before. Going forward, the cost of opposition would be that "your wife will become a widow, your children will become orphans, and your mother will have to give birth to another person to replace you after your death." It soon became clear that Boko Haram had both the will and the resources to carry out these threats.[20]

A Nation in Crisis

Violence Rising

About a month after the prison break, Boko Haram staged another round of attacks that offered important clues about its future intentions. On October 6, 2010, gunmen on motorcycles followed two leading Borno politicians to their residences in Maiduguri. At the home of the speaker of the State House of Assembly, the gunmen were driven off, but they succeeded in assassinating the state chairman of Sheriff's All Nigeria Peoples' Party (ANPP). On the 9th, shooters gunned down a local Muslim cleric outside his home. Over the next few months, the group claimed credit for a series of attacks targeting various arms of the Nigerian government and religious figures who opposed Yusuf's theology.

Meanwhile, Boko Haram spokesmen gave interviews to the local media, promising an end to the violence in exchange for releasing the group's members from detention, the opportunity to return to their communities and mosques, and Sheriff's resignation. Local journalists readily grasped the significance of these demands, pointing to Borno's dysfunctional politics, the government's failure to act earlier to stem Yusuf's influence, and the continued problems of poverty and inequality as obvious factors in the group's reemergence. The official responses, however, were mostly punitive. There were troop movements, deployments of armored vehicles and helicopters, and expensive new purchases to beef up local security forces.

In December 2010, the "new" Boko Haram launched its first major attack outside the northeast, a series of marketplace bombings on Christmas Eve in Jos. Jos is the capital of Plateau State, an area long known for its natural beauty and a diverse and multiethnic populace. Founded in 1915 as a mining town, it became a cosmopolitan center at the heart of what is called the "Middle Belt" of Nigeria, where people from all over the country have settled for economic opportunities. However, despite Jos's cosmopolitan culture, it has also been troubled by ethnic and religious crises since as early as 1945, when it was the site of Nigeria's first-ever ethnic crisis between Hausa and Igbo traders. Since that time, many of the crises have been between the mostly Christian Berom ethnic community (who claim to be the region's original indigenes) and the predominantly Muslim Hausa and Fulani groups who have settled there over the past several centuries. Since the return to civilian rule in 1999, protests over potential implementation of shari'ah and contentious local elections have contributed to a massive spike in communal violence across the state and especially in Jos itself.

From the beginning, effective responses to Boko Haram's violence have been hampered by a political culture that encourages politicians and even ordinary citizens to see its actions in terms of existing local conflicts. In the wake of the Christmas Eve attack (amplified by a series of coordinated bombings of Christian churches in Maiduguri), some local Christians in Jos responded by retaliating against their Muslim neighbors. Meanwhile, local political and religious leaders on both sides scrambled to fit the attacks into self-serving narratives that blamed their opponents rather than Boko Haram. Prominent Muslim leaders hinted that the attacks were a Christian plot to stir up ethnoreligious tensions, while supporters of Plateau State's Christian governor, Jonah Jang, portrayed them as the work of Muslim politicians seeking to undermine his administration.

In late 2010, Boko Haram also made its first strike on Abuja, with a New Year's Eve bombing at a small market outside an army barracks. A second cluster of coordinated attacks in Abuja, Bauchi, and Zaria coincided with the inauguration of newly elected President Goodluck Jonathan on May 29, 2011. Whatever Boko Haram's intentions, these attacks invited ethnoreligious political tensions into the security conversation, making it more difficult to adopt a unified plan to stop what by now had become a national emergency. The post-election riots that swept northern cities such as Kano and Zaria, attacking northern politicians who had supported Jonathan's candidacy, made it harder still.

The first hint that something worse was coming arrived on June 16, 2011, when Boko Haram mounted Nigeria's first-ever reported suicide bombing, on the national police headquarters in Abuja. As AFP correspondent Mike Smith reported, the attack itself was largely a failure. The bomb detonated while the perpetrator's car was at a security checkpoint just inside the headquarters gate, and while two police officers were killed and more than seventy cars destroyed, it failed to damage the convoy of national police chief Hafiz Ringim.[1]

Despite the bombing's failure, a message released afterward threatened ominously that some of its members had recently brought back new tactics from their time training with the Somali al-Qaeda affiliate al-Shabaab. For his part, Salkida secured an interview with a reputed Boko Haram spokesman who provided details such as the bomber's identity (a former follower of Yusuf's), the fact that they had provided a cash payout to his widows and children, and that—most importantly—they had as many as one hundred "screened" volunteers ready for future attacks.[2]

On August 26, 2011, a suicide bomber penetrated the security of the United Nations (UN) building in Abuja's diplomatic zone, killing twenty-three people, including more than a dozen UN employees. For many outside Nigeria, this was their first exposure to the group. Reporting on the attack also revealed just how little was known about Boko Haram outside of northeastern Nigeria. The international press noted that the group had made few demands other than "justice" for its fallen and imprisoned members and that it lacked a clear manifesto beyond a desire for greater adherence to shari'ah and a dislike of Nigeria's democratic institutions.

An SSS report eventually identified Mamman Nur, a member of Yusuf's inner circle—and allegedly the man who had introduced Yusuf to Shekau—as the "mastermind" of the attack. Nur is one of the most shadowy figures in the Boko Haram world. Media reports based on a combination of SSS statements and sources "claiming to have been sect members as well as those familiar with the group" claimed that Nur had briefly led the postuprising Boko Haram while Shekau recovered from his injuries, engaged in (and lost) an internal power struggle, and then fled the country. They also repeated claims that he had spent his nearly two years away in Somalia, training with al-Shabaab and developing the technical know-how for more deadly attacks.[3]

In response, the Jonathan administration announced that Boko Haram would be the administration's "priority item" but offered little in the way of a more definitive commitment. Nor did there seem to be much desire to look inward, despite disturbing evidence that Boko Haram's successes were abetted by the corruption and decay that had plagued Nigeria's security services for decades. Indeed, in an interview with Salkida, the infamous Boko Haram spokesman "Abu Qaqa" claimed that the bomber and his collaborators had transported the explosives all the way from Maiduguri by road, paying off officers at various checkpoints as they went.[4]

In a little less than a year, Boko Haram had evolved from the remnants of the Maiduguri uprising into a capable fighting force. Again, it is difficult to say how much of this was driven by ties to the transnational jihadist community. As Mike Smith noted, perhaps the biggest difference between the UN bombing and its less deadly predecessors was not the bomb's design or delivery mechanism—something Nur and others might have been trained in—but that they had learned from their previous failures to ram the building's more lightly defended exit gate instead of the main entrance.[5] What is more certain was that the UN bombing marked the end of Boko Haram's second phase. From here, both the group and the state response to it would become deadlier, putting all of Nigeria—but especially Borno State—on a war footing, with devastating consequences.

Factions and Factionalism

Although bombing government buildings makes headlines, Boko Haram's death toll has been built primarily through attacks against civilians in public places. Expanding on the bloody success of their 2010 Christmas bombings and a string of attacks on Christian churches, the group's tactics shifted increasingly during the second half of 2011 and on into 2012 toward soft targets that included mosques, Muslim clerics, and traditional rulers. This new strategy—along with Shekau's increasingly visible role as the group's mastermind—revealed previously hidden divisions.

There has been a great deal of speculation about the nature of Boko Haram's internal organization. Early reports pointed to evidence of a "cell" structure, with representatives in places such as Kano operating independently of Shekau's leadership. Interviews with group members and former participants conducted by the International Crisis Group suggested that they were split into as many as six distinct factions, defined by a combination of leadership schisms and geographic divisions. Other assessments proposed that there were at least four "versions" of Boko Haram actively engaged in violence, including the core ideologues of Yusuf's movement, criminal gangs using the Boko Haram "brand," thugs sponsored by political actors, and even rogue members of the army and police using the violence as cover for their corrupt dealings.

A simpler explanation is that Boko Haram's leadership was (and remains) deeply divided over what exactly it was fighting for. This conflict has its earliest roots in the alleged power struggle between Shekau and Nur following Yusuf's death. As one (clearly biased but interesting) source—*Al-Risalah* magazine, a publication produced by the Syrian al-Qaeda affiliate Nusra Front—described it in a January 2017 piece, the core issue was Shekau's claim that all Nigerian Muslims who participate in state institutions such as government-run schools and elections were unbelievers and thus fair targets. While *takfir* (the act of declaring other Muslims "unbelievers" as a result of their actions or beliefs) is a core part of Salafi theology, Shekau's claim went far beyond not only anything previously heard in Nigeria but also beyond even what groups such as al-Qaeda and ISIS have generally endorsed. Shekau's position soon proved extreme even among extremists, alienating potential supporters at home and abroad.

The first Boko Haram supporters to break away from Shekau's leadership were among those with the strongest connections to the world of global jihad. In late January 2012, a pamphlet circulated in Kano announcing a new organization called Jama'atu Ansaril Muslimina fi Biladis Sudan (roughly, "Vanguard for the Protection of Muslims in Sub-Saharan Africa"), or Ansaru for short. Ansaru was a small group, built around the leadership of a handful of foreign-trained Nigerian jihadists who had originally fallen in with Yusuf in the mid-2000s but maintained their ties in Algeria and Mali. In effect, it operated as a de facto AQIM franchise in northern Nigeria and Cameroon.

Ansaru's leadership vehemently criticized Shekau's willingness to kill fellow Muslims. Yet despite these concerns, Ansaru leaders often worked with him anyway when money was on the line. Throughout 2012 and 2013, the group played a key role in several large attacks, including the kidnappings of a handful of European expatriate workers. It is likely that they strategically allowed Shekau's Boko Haram to take credit (and benefit financially) for some of these in exchange for certain concessions, while others were revenue-sharing operations in which Ansaru provided the tactical know-how and Boko Haram the security.[6] Since 2014, however, the group appears defunct, with many of its most important members either captured by Nigerian forces or reintegrated into the larger organization.

Money has also sometimes driven Boko Haram's factions apart. In May 2011, assailants kidnapped a pair of European engineers, Chris McManus and Franco Lamolinara, from a work site near Birnin Kebbi, a mid-sized city in northwestern Nigeria. Kidnapping for ransom has long been an important tactic for AQIM and its Sahelian affiliates, raising significant revenue (one credible estimate puts the number at $89 million as of 2012 alone) for other operations. And across Nigeria, criminal gangs regularly kidnap public figures and their family members for quick ransom payments, usually returning their victims unharmed. Yet at the time, Boko Haram had no track record of ransom kidnappings. It is widely believed that most of their biggest financial successes in the early days of the kidnapping business—the (at least) $3.5 million they grossed from the kidnapping of French citizens and the wife of a leading politician in Cameroon in 2013, for example—were actually run by Ansaru or other outsiders.

As American security analyst Jacob Zenn has argued, it was unclear from the beginning whether Boko

Haram was even involved in the McManus and Lamolinara kidnapping. Three "proof of life" videos were released in the name of "al-Qaeda in the Lands Beyond the Sahel," a group that seems to have been created out of whole cloth for this operation. The videos were sent to and released not via Boko Haram's usual channels but via a government media source in Mauritania that had previously received other AQIM-sponsored announcements, and Shekau was notably absent. And, of course, the entire plot was carried out more than 1,100 kilometers from Boko Haram's Borno homeland.[7]

Details eventually came to light in March 2012, following an unsuccessful rescue attempt by a joint force of Nigerian and British commandos during which both captives perished. Days before the ill-fated mission, Nigerian operatives staged their own raid on a safe house in Zaria, arresting the alleged mastermind, a previously unknown figure named "Abu Mohammed." Mohammed, who later died in custody, seems to have been connected to Ansaru leaders, and most sources agree that his "group" had relied on training and material support from AQIM and its allies.

More troubling allegations revolved around Mohammed's relationship with Shekau and their plans for the anticipated €5 million ransom. After the botched rescue, a Boko Haram spokesman disavowed any involvement in the kidnapping, while leaks from the state security services suggested that the confidential informants who had revealed Mohammed's base were actually Shekau's men. Inside sources reported that British and Italian officials had been engaged in ransom talks for nearly a year with representatives of what they believed to be AQIM. It has been widely speculated that a revenue-sharing arrangement between Shekau's forces and the kidnappers once existed but that by the spring of 2012 it had broken down, leading them to sell out their erstwhile allies. That Boko Haram factions were using the police and military to carry out retaliation against each other spoke not only to the depth of the schism but also to the security services' lack of a broader strategic understanding of how the group was organized and operated.[8]

Yet another piece of evidence came from the same story (and the same intelligence) that alleged Mamman Nur's role in the UN bombing. Unnamed Nigerian intelligence sources reported that the conflict between Nur and Shekau was far from settled and that Boko Haram "chieftains" had their own bases of support, allowing them to operate independently. The bombshell was the claim (never fully confirmed or disconfirmed) that Shekau had not personally signed off on the UN attack. Leaked reports from the interrogation of Kabiru Sokoto, a Boko Haram lieutenant convicted of masterminding a Christmas Day church bombing near Abuja in 2011, revealed a group filled with "distrust and acrimony." Sokoto allegedly revealed that Shekau exercised nearly total unilateral control over the organization's finances, even over money earmarked for the widows and families of his fallen troops. Yet "no one dared ask questions for fear of death," an accusation that has been repeatedly leveled at Shekau by his opponents, who paint him as adept at violently purging anyone in the group who challenged him.[9]

Perhaps not surprisingly, these conflicts are quite common within terrorist groups. Al-Qaeda, for example, is famous for a number of long-running feuds between its top ideologues and commanders, focused not only on weighty issues of strategy and theology but also on mundane problems of expense reporting and recordkeeping. Yet even by these standards, Boko Haram's divisions seem exceptional. Shekau's leadership was at the root of a massive schism that played out in August 2016, when an ISIS publication announced that it recognized Abu Musab al-Barnawi, Mohammed Yusuf's son, as the "governor" of IS's West African franchise, the so-called Islamic State in West Africa (ISWAP). Although the announcement did not mention Shekau by name, this was a coup. Shekau quickly disseminated his own audio message that acknowledged his split with IS but insisted that he remained in charge of the broader movement.

US intelligence sources suggested that these tensions had been simmering for some time. In June 2016, the commander of United States Africa Command speculated publicly that perhaps as many as half of Boko Haram's fighting force had already broken away from the main body as a result of Shekau's unwillingness to "buy into" the alliance with ISIS, including its insistence that Boko Haram reduce civilian casualties and stop using children as bombers. And Barnawi's own statement, released days after Shekau's, accused him of presiding over a "caliphate of injustice," ordering the deaths of dozens of fighters over trivial offenses while neglecting to procure food for the group's children or weapons and ammunition for its fighters. As of mid-2018, the two factions were operating largely independently of each other, with ISWAP's forces mostly in the far northeast corner of Borno State near the Nigerien and Chadian borders, on the islands of Lake Chad, and stretching into Yobe State, while Shekau's loyalists operated primarily in a large swath of southern Borno State.

Fighting Back?

In September 2011, former US ambassador to Nigeria John Campbell penned a short essay on the Nigerian government's counterterrorism activities titled "To Battle Boko Haram, Put Down Your Guns." It was one of the first serious international acknowledgements that the Jonathan administration's aimless, military-heavy response to the violence might be part of the problem. As Campbell described it, there were two main issues. The first was that the Nigerian security services had failed to learn from their role in facilitating Boko Haram's creation. Indeed, during the aftermath of a marketplace bombing in Maiduguri on July 23, 2011, members of the Joint Task Force (JTF, an infamous and now-disbanded joint military-police security unit) had responded by killing civilians on the scene and burning down the market.

The other was that the administration still lacked a comprehensive plan. The election that had brought Jonathan to power had been both procedurally suspect and marked by violence, particularly in the same northern communities now fearful of Boko Haram's growing reach. Yet Campbell argued that the new administration had done little to reach across the traditional ethnic and religious aisles of Nigerian politics, allowing the perception (if not the reality) of the north's marginalization to alienate potential allies in civil society, government, and even the general population.[10]

The administration's uncertainty was matched by a broader social divide. In some quarters, there was support for negotiations with willing Boko Haram members, perhaps culminating in an amnesty program for those who agreed to lay down their arms. Their reference was the Presidential Amnesty Programme (PAP) created in June 2009, which provided total amnesty for militants in the Niger Delta region. The conflict there, which pits members of minority ethnic communities who have suffered the environmental ravages of the region's oil production against the federal government, saw the proliferation of regional militias that damaged pipelines, kidnapped oil workers, and massively disrupted Nigeria's key economic sector. PAP offered youth participants the opportunity to turn in their weapons in exchange for access to job-training opportunities and monthly cash payments and ultimately demobilized more than thirty thousand fighters.

To be clear, PAP has not been an unmitigated success. It has struggled to gain local legitimacy, fighting the perception that it was meant not to restore communities but to ensure oil revenues for state elites and multinational corporations. Still, the prospect of ending violence has repeatedly brought the government to the negotiating table, and there have been concerted efforts to adopt a similar strategy with Boko Haram. The first effort, a committee appointed by Jonathan in July 2011, disbanded because it could not find a credible counterpart on the Boko Haram side. In March 2012, another attempt broke down when the government's mediator, a leading Muslim civil-society leader requested by Boko Haram's leadership, quit after the content of his discussions were leaked to the media. And in October 2014, government officials announced a cease-fire, only to have it revealed weeks later, following a series of deadly attacks, that they had been negotiating with someone who had no contact with Shekau. More damning than these failures, however, are allegations that at least two different efforts to negotiate for the release of the Chibok abductees—including one begun only weeks after their kidnapping—collapsed due to a lack of planning and interagency cooperation. These failures, and the eventual payout of €3 million—money that the group likely used to stage a rash of suicide attacks in 2017—for the return of 103 of the girls in October 2016 and May 2017 speak to the difficulty of mounting a cash-for-peace plan without a peace plan in place.

Geography is another complication. Despite attacks in places such as Kano, Abuja, and Jos, Boko Haram's impact outside its home region has been limited. Shekau took credit in June 2014 for a pair of explosions in a fuel depot in Lagos, Nigeria's largest city and its economic hub, but journalists and researchers have been unable to verify the government's claims that it frequently arrests suspects and breaks up terrorist cells in the southern half of the country. Public opinion outside the northeast showed significantly less public concern about Boko Haram or fear that violent military reprisals might actually make the conflict worse. A national phone survey conducted in 2011 found that a plurality of Nigerians (44 percent) supported a military solution to Boko Haram's attacks, while 68 percent supported strengthening the national security apparatus. And a 2013 survey found that more than 70 percent of Nigerians felt that the conflict had not impacted them personally, including 88 percent of those in the country's southwestern area, home to Lagos.[11] Anecdotally, many southern Nigerians regard Boko Haram as a "northern" problem, a self-inflicted wound caused by the region's own politicians' meddling with religion and for it to resolve on its own.

On December 31, 2011, the Jonathan administration issued the first of two "state of emergency" declarations covering Boko Haram's northeastern homeland. The first targeted a handful of local government areas, while the second, in May 2013, covered all of Borno, Yobe, and Adamawa States. Both called for security forces to ramp up their efforts to disrupt Boko Haram's activities, deny it recruits and resources, and decapitate its leadership. But, as human rights activists have pointed out, Jonathan's order that security forces take "all necessary action" to destroy Boko Haram seems to have been understood by many within the military to mean that if ending the conflict required increased civilian casualties and "collateral damage," so be it. Over the half-decade that followed, international human rights activists, journalists, and local residents have documented an extraordinarily wide and brutal range of human rights abuses by Nigerian security forces against civilians, including extrajudicial executions of suspects on a scale that exceeds even the Yusuf incident.

The most thorough accounting of Nigerian military and police practices during the war, released by Amnesty International, estimates that, from 2011 to 2015, government forces arrested *at least* twenty thousand people. Some were certainly genuine participants in Boko Haram's violence, while others offered support to the group in some way or another. But as Amnesty and others have documented, the bulk seem to have been young men and boys in the wrong place at the wrong time, caught up in a system that lacked the skill or resources to separate real perpetrators from the general population. The absence of a centralized tracking system meant that while some detainees were cleared within a few days, others were held indefinitely without charges, access to legal counsel, or even a word to their families. Prosecutions were infrequent, and whatever evidence the government possessed about these "suspects" was rarely made public.[12]

That the Nigerian police and armed forces would engage in systematic violence against the communities they are meant to protect is tragic but not shocking. Nigerian police officials, politicians, and community leaders often endorse violence against criminal suspects and prisoners as a means of controlling crime. And whatever other lessons the country may have learned from its decades of rule by the military, it continues to play a major role in internal security operations. When Nigerian security forces find themselves in a dangerous situation, they often escalate it. As remarkable data from the Nigeria Watch project suggests, from 2006 to 2014, the Nigerian Police Force killed someone 58 percent of the time when responding to a violent incident. For comparison's sake, in the United States, a country with its own serious problems with police violence, official statistics suggest that less than half a percent of violent encounters between police and the public end in an arrest-related death.[13]

In March 2012, Bishop Ayo Oritsejafor, a popular and charismatic Christian pastor and the president of the Christian Association of Nigeria (CAN), one of the country's largest religious-interest groups, made a now infamous claim that the federal government was "pampering" alleged members of Boko Haram in police custody. The reality could not have been more different. Even official military field reports acknowledged at least a thousand civilians have died in military custody, while Amnesty's estimate, based on mortuary records, interviews, and leaked internal reports, was over seven thousand. At one military-run prison in Adamawa State, it gathered testimony alleging systematic torture and abuse, including prisoners beaten with water hoses and confined to spaces so small and overcrowded they could not lie down. Another source alleged that many were denied food and water at the insistence of the barracks commander and that the bodies of the dead were rarely returned to their families for burial lest they make public complaints about their condition.

The most notorious detention center is Giwa Barracks in Maiduguri, where one high-ranking military source estimated that as many as five thousand died in 2013 and 2014 alone. There military police allegedly held more than one thousand prisoners in a single cell measuring approximately 200 square meters, without access to toilets or showers, feeding them starvation rations while cholera outbreaks and other diseases decimated their ranks. Former detainees often reported that, out of the dozens of men they had been arrested with, only a handful survived. And after Boko Haram staged a daring attack on the barracks in March 2014, Amnesty obtained video and photographic evidence that 640 escapees were recaptured and systematically executed, their bodies hidden in at least three mass graves. And perhaps worst of all, in May 2016, nearly a year after President Buhari promised investigations into Amnesty's initial allegations, it was documenting the deaths of babies detained along with their mothers in Giwa.

Detention centers have not been the only place where civilians have faced state-sponsored violence. In April 2013, a military patrol responding to an attack by Boko Haram fighters near the town of Baga in Borno State retaliated by destroying over two thousand homes and buildings in civilian neighborhoods, an act confirmed by satellite photography obtained by Human Rights Watch. And in February 2015 and January 2017, Nigerian Air Force operations went badly wrong, killing dozens of mourners gathered at a mosque just over the Niger border and 115 internally displaced people in a government-run camp near the village of Rann, respectively. In the case of the 2015 bombing raid, Nigerian defense ministry spokesman General Chris Olukolade not only failed to apologize for the tragic error but also took to Twitter to accuse troops from Niger of corruption, cowardice in battle, and even collaboration with Boko Haram.

Nigerians have responded to these atrocities in a variety of ways. Some journalists and civil-society organizations have launched their own investigations, even as they face the prospect of harassment or arrest by the federal government. Others have alleged, perhaps not entirely unfairly, that there is an important measure of hypocrisy in Western condemnations of civilian deaths in the fight against terrorism in the Global South when the human cost of the US war on terror has been so high for the civilians of Iraq, Afghanistan, and elsewhere. The late Nigerian ambassador to the United States, Adebowale Adefuye, publicly alleged in 2014 that the United States' reluctance to provide weapons and military technology on the basis of "rumors, hearsays, and exaggerated accounts" of human rights abuses was, in effect, responsible for the civilian and military deaths inflicted by Boko Haram. As of 2018, the relationship had been thawed somewhat by the Trump administration's support for—and final approval of—a set of twelve A-29 Super Tucano light attack aircraft intended for the fight against Boko Haram, a sale that had been delayed under the Obama administrations by the Nigerian military's repeated accidental bombing of civilian targets. At nearly $500 million, it was the largest single arms sale ever between the two countries.

Civilians to the Rescue?

By 2013, few communities affected by Boko Haram had much faith in their military's ability to protect them. In June, disparate groups of civilians who had taken it upon themselves to man checkpoints and patrol around Maiduguri consolidated into a single body, which came to be called the Civilian Joint Task Force, or CJTF. These vigilantes, sometimes called *'yan goro,* or "men with sticks," are lightly armed. Few have military weapons, and most wield little more than their eponymous sticks, machetes, bows, or locally made hunting rifles called "Dane guns," yet they are key players in the fight against Boko Haram.

Although they are officially independent, from the beginning the CJTF has had (as the name suggests) a close relationship with the state security forces. Indeed, the JTF played a central role in helping the nascent group organize and recruit and encouraged it to set up a leadership structure that would be friendly to coordination with the military. The Borno State government also saw the appeal and has not only provided limited support and resources (including uniforms and vehicles but not weapons) but has even encouraged its officials to join in leadership roles as well. It also set up its own program, the Borno Youths Empowerment Scheme, which recruited, trained, and even provided stipends for nearly two thousand young men mobilized into the CJTF.

Internationally, the CJTF's efforts often receive uncritical praise. Media coverage tends to latch onto unique stories about the ordinary men and women who have taken the fight to Boko Haram, while paying little attention to the broader complexities of asking civilians to become ad hoc combatants against one of the world's deadliest insurgencies. Take, for example, the story of Aisha Bakari Gombi, a resident of the infamous Sambisa Forest area recruited by a local military unit to act as a guide and "hunter" across this difficult and isolated terrain, with its broad mix of open forest and dense vegetation. Located southeast of Maiduguri, it had been maintained as a game reserve since colonial times until it was taken over by Boko Haram. Numerous media reports have cast Gombi and others like her as unlikely heroes, an indispensable resource in the military's efforts to root out Boko Haram fighters from their hiding places, while saying little about the underlying conditions that made her participation necessary.

On the positive side, the CJTF and other vigilante efforts have had a real, positive impact on the conflict. While there is no way to definitively measure this impact, the bulk of it has come in the form of improved intelligence-gathering and relations with local communities. The structure of the Nigerian military and police—both federal agencies commanded from Abuja—has long meant that the day-to-day work of securing Nigeria's vulnerable communities falls to soldiers and police officers who lack a personal connection to them and who often share neither the local language or religion. The CJTF's ability to understand the local terrain—to recognize new faces, notice what is out of place, and perceive possible threats—hearkens back to a precolonial security system, in which local emirs and other traditional leaders could rely on a dense network of officials and informants to prevent potential social disruptions. In both urban Maiduguri and rural, isolated pockets of the hinterland, the CJTF has played a key role in limiting Boko Haram's ability to operate without detection and impediment.

These benefits have also come with costs. One is that despite its greater connection to the communities they defend, the CJTF has also been credibly accused of extrajudicial violence. CJTF members have been documented participating in the execution of suspects alongside members of the military, and the military has allegedly passed on detainees to the CJTF for interrogation in order to insulate themselves from evidence of torture. There is also evidence that vigilantes used familiar tactics to shake down community members at roadblocks and that when their members commit crimes—including sexual violence—against civilians, they are rarely held accountable.

Then there is Boko Haram itself, which has been quite direct about how it escalated violence against communities that supported vigilante forces. In no small part because the Nigerian military has been (rightly) reluctant to arm the CJTF over fears that the weapons would end up in Boko Haram's hands, the vigilantes have rarely been able to defend themselves from full-scale attacks. In Borno, the death toll for vigilantes has exceeded six hundred. It is also likely that many CJTF members choose to participate for reasons more complicated than heroism. Interviews with CJTF leaders suggest that the group was formed not only to fight Boko Haram but also to combat the military's own indiscriminate targeting of civilians and reprisal attacks on communities perceived as harboring Boko Haram sympathies.[14]

In all, by early 2017, there were "officially" twenty-six thousand CJTF members in Borno State alone, and local observers estimate that the total number of vigilantes across northeastern Nigeria have been double that. But while the conflict appears (as of this writing) to be far from over, the question of what will happen when it is remains. As nearly all research on postconflict environments suggests, once irregular fighters have been armed and mobilized, it is hard to put the genie back in the bottle. As Borno State governor Kashim Shettima noted in December 2015, the problems likely to face CJTF members once the conflict is over are the same as those that created the context for Boko Haram's creation in the first place: "unemployment, illiteracy, hunger, and extreme poverty." Without a plan in place, he suggested, the CJTF risks becoming the "Frankenstein monster that might end up consuming us all."[15]

Chibok and the War on Women

Ironically, the CJTF's efforts to root out Boko Haram supporters in Maiduguri played a key role in the expanded violence to come. During the summer of 2013, CJTF efforts succeeded in driving most Boko Haram fighters out of the city, forcing them to regroup by establishing a network of rural hideouts in the Sambisa Forest. This displacement, along with Shekau's increasingly influential ideological commitment to takfir, would have long-term consequences for the group's evolving tactics and strategic plans.

Although the group had begun attacking civilians alongside state actors relatively early on, the move to the countryside pushed it further away from terrorist tactics and toward an increasingly full-scale military presence designed to quickly attack lightly defended targets far from military installations. In the early morning on July 6, 2013, gunmen staged an attack on a boarding school in the town of Mamudo in Yobe State. They eventually set fire to the campus, shooting anyone able to escape the flames. In all, more than forty students and teachers died. Over the next few months, they staged a series of raids on other schools and college campuses with increasingly bloody success.

As journalists at the time often took pains to note, most of the victims of these school attacks were young Muslim men. But as early as 2011, Boko Haram had also begun to target a handful of communities in southern Borno with larger Christian populations. The best-known of these is, of course, Chibok. Chibok's history has some important resonances with the current situation. Chibok's indigenous residents and their neighbors have a long history of pushing back against the efforts of regional powers such as the Borno Empire to dominate them. And like other minority ethnic communities scattered among the region's remote hills, mountains, and forest reserves, they were often the targets of slave raids by Muslim traders. Beginning in the 1920s, US-based missionaries entered the area, and slowly over the course of several generations many members of the community converted to Christianity, sending their children to newly founded mission schools. This included the very secondary school from which the girls would be abducted, which had been operated by the Church of the Brethren (a US-based Protestant denomination that later came to be known in Nigeria as the Ekklesiyar Yan'uwa a Nigeria, or EYN) until it was turned over to the government in the 1970s.

A second and perhaps even more important shift in Boko Haram's strategy was its decision, likely sometime in early 2013, to begin targeting women and girls. The first abductions took place during attacks in urban centers such as Maiduguri and Damaturu, although fighters soon carried the strategy into the countryside. At first Boko Haram portrayed these abductions as reprisals, either against families who had not supported the group or authorities who had detained the wives and families of group members. But much as with the attacks against schools and Christian-majority communities, it soon became apparent that the group's ambitions were broader. By 2016, most estimates put the number of women abducted at least two thousand.

At various times, both Boko Haram and its former captives have provided different accounts of why these particular women were targets. Was it because, as so many international activists have framed it, they had dared to go to (Western) schools? Was it because, as Shekau himself has claimed more than once, Boko Haram's fight is fundamentally with Christians and other manifestations of Western culture, or because the girls were intended as slaves for the group, wives for its members, and a potential bargaining chip in potential negotiations? Or perhaps, as secret diaries kept by some of the Chibok abductees during their captivity suggest, was it a spur-of-the-moment decision, taken only after the building equipment the group had originally come for could not be found?

Boko Haram's violence against women fits into a long legacy of patriarchy and women's marginalization throughout the region. Although there are important examples of powerful female leaders and scholars in precolonial northern Nigerian history, many ordinary women faced kidnapping for ransom, enslavement, and concubinage within the slave economy of the Sokoto Caliphate and its neighbors. Well into the twenty-first century, northern women remain profoundly unrepresented in and poorly served by the Nigerian government. Muslim religious and political elites have staunchly refused to support legislation to set eighteen as the minimum age of marital consent, and regional fertility rates are above six births per woman. Illiteracy rates are nearly 30 percent higher among women than men, and in Borno State fewer than 5 percent of school-aged girls complete primary school. Women who are today the victims of Boko Haram were not accorded the right to vote until the mid-1970s and rarely hold elected office.

At the same time, movements such as Izala attract widespread support from Muslim women, in no small part because they promote women's access to education, state policies that promote marriage by covering traditional bride-price and dowry costs, and uphold the religious duty of husbands to care for their families. Yusuf's movement was no different. While he preached severe restrictions on women's access to public spaces, he also encouraged marriage within the community and helped male followers start businesses that would allow their new spouses to avoid harsh domestic labor and to live lives of relative luxury (benefits that seems to have continued for the wives of favored Boko Haram commanders).

As the conflict intensified through 2012 and 2013, Boko Haram focused on recruiting, controlling, and dominating women, their bodies, and their work in service of their cause. American security analysts Mia Bloom and Hilary Matfess argue that Boko Haram came to view women as having two primary roles: "swords" who provide crucial support to the fight, either by dealing directly in violence or (more often) as slaves and servants; and "symbols" who provide the group an opportunity to demonstrate their piety and commitment to shari'ah. For Christians, like the majority of the Chibok abductees (who were reportedly isolated from other female captives and sometimes received "special" treatment), their role as "symbols" meant enforced religious education and pressure to convert to Islam and adopt the group's ideology, including (as some sources suggest) their embrace of violence. For hundreds of others, their daily lives were filled with a combination of systematic rape and forced servitude, as they were forced to perform the work (sexual and domestic) that Shekau and other leaders saw as essential to maintaining the insurgency.[16]

Although data is scarce, most analysts believe that the majority of women involved in the conflict were coerced into participation, and even those who joined "willingly" faced indirect pressure from their families ("voluntary" recruits often report having a brother, husband, or parent participating in the group). Yet it is clear from interviews with women who have escaped or been "liberated" from the group that, for some, their participation involved elements of choice and agency. As Matfess documents through interviews with dozens of female former participants, women who joined Boko Haram did so for a range of reasons. Some, particularly the daughters, sisters, and wives of group members (or alleged members) killed by government forces were fueled by grievance and a desire for justice, and there is some indication that these women are among the most likely to not only choose a life with the group but also volunteer as suicide bombers. Others had reached marriageable age, and the most attractive suitor (either to them or their family) was a Boko Haram member. And a few, particularly the former wives of Boko Haram commanders, tell a story about how the group provided their dowries, offered them a life free from hard agricultural work, and promised social status through the visible piety of their seclusion. These women describe doting husbands who returned from raids and attacks with houseware, clothing, and makeup, as well as the power and status their powerful spouses provided among the group's women. Others who joined by marrying less prestigious fighters (or who were abducted into the group and subsequently forcibly married) faced significantly harsher burdens.[17]

Boko Haram's massive deployment of female bombers raises yet more questions about how to parse issues of victimhood and agency in women's participation in the insurgency. Indeed, Boko Haram holds the tragic distinction of having deployed more female bombers (at least 244 as of June 2017, more than half of all of the group's bombers) than any other terrorist group in history by a significant margin. What does this tell us? A 2017 report of the US Military Academy's Combatting Terrorism Center argues that while the group's choice to use so many women and children bombers is undoubtedly tactically advantageous (they are difficult to detect), it is also driven by symbolic concerns. It also finds that, on average, attacks carried out by women are significantly less fatal, driving down the group's overall "success" rate in comparison to other groups that deploy mostly male bombers. Female bombers are also more likely to be directed at "soft" civilian targets such as markets and other public spaces, whereas male bombers are more likely to strike military or governmental targets. The report concludes that, in light of this evidence, it is likely that Boko Haram's real goal is to attract media coverage and global attention, as well as to drive fear of women in public spaces.[18]

Moreover, the very nature of successful suicide attacks makes it difficult to determine exactly how many participants were recruited willingly or not. As Matfess argues, when women who spent time willingly with the group are asked about Boko Haram's violence against civilians or its use of suicide bombers, they give incomplete and unsatisfactory answers, emphasizing their ignorance of what their husbands were doing or evading culpability by attributing the group's actions to "divine will."[19] Meanwhile, evidence from arrested would-be bombers, some of whom alerted the authorities and requested that their suicide vests be removed, finds that some had been coerced by family members or captors or sexually and psychologically abused, while others—particularly the youngest—did not seem to understand their mission or its intended result. Yet nearly all women who survive captivity (or worse) by Boko Haram face the prospect of discrimination or even retaliatory violence when they return home, as few there are sure how to differentiate (if it is even possible) between "real" victims and sympathizers.

Nowhere is this stigma clearer than in the northeast's sprawling camps for internally displaced persons (IDPs). Although accurate statistics are hard to come by, women made up a clear majority of IDPs living in government-run camps in 2016. Here they have faced malnutrition, lack of medical care, and an appalling death rate for their young children. They have also confronted continued sexual violence, as documented in persistent reports of camp workers and security officers demanding sex for access to scarce food and medical care. There is also evidence of a worrying trend of poor displaced families "selling" their daughters into marriage in order to collect the bride-price, a practice that often leads not only to sexual exploitation but also divorce and further stigma for the young women involved. Even optimistic news, such as the proliferation of women's empowerment programs to help orphaned or widowed IDPs gain a measure of economic independence, has been marred by resistance from men who claim that women are being given "favorable" treatment by nongovernmental organization (NGO) workers and government officials.

"The Size of Belgium"

The failure of the Nigerian government's response to the Chibok abductions was, in retrospect, just one of many important signs that the conflict was about to become much worse. Another was a precipitous decline in military morale, as frontline soldiers and security officers became increasingly disgruntled, frustrated, and even unwilling to fight. Less than a month after Chibok, Amnesty International reported evidence that military officials in Maiduguri had word of the impending attack four hours before it was launched but that they failed to reinforce the small local garrison. Testimony heard by Amnesty placed part of the blame on a lack of resources but also a growing reluctance among the troops charged with protecting threatened communities to actually fight Boko Haram, which they believed to be better armed and commanded.

Soon, other troubling reports of further dissension in the ranks trickled out of Maiduguri. In May 2014, there were two incidents at Maimalari Barracks, headquarters of the Nigerian Army's Seventh Infantry Division, where troops protested delays in their salary payments by physically challenging officers and shooting into the air. In August, soldiers returning from a high-casualty engagement near Gwoza shot at the front gates of their barracks, demanding an explanation for why they had not been given the manpower and firepower necessary to defend themselves. Soon after, fifty-nine soldiers were arrested and convicted for refusing to deploy to the front, part of a larger group of court-martial cases intended to reestablish order in the ranks. The month ended with more than four hundred troops crossing over the border into Cameroon and refusing to return. Although military spokesmen later claimed the soldiers had crossed the border in pursuit of Boko Haram fighters, it took a heavily guarded convoy to bring them back home.

Meanwhile, empowered by their successes against isolated and poorly defended targets, Boko Haram began to stage larger-scale and more complex operations, eventually seizing control of much of the Borno countryside away from an ill-prepared Nigerian military. These successes in turn helped further broaden the group's horizons. Dating back to the days of the so-called Nigerian Taliban, the porous and lightly defended borders of Niger, Chad, and Cameroon had long served as escape valves for fighters facing pressure from Nigerian troops, and there is evidence that Boko Haram had been quietly operating across all three borders for some time, perhaps even with the tacit acknowledgement of local authorities. But as the insurgents' presence grew, so did their ambitions, and by early 2015, northern Cameroon had become a full-fledged front in the war, with raids on villages up and down the border providing key supplies and new recruits to sustain the fight elsewhere.

In August 2014, Boko Haram fighters overran and occupied the city of Gwoza. Nestled in the foothills of the Mandara Mountains and 130 kilometers southeast of Maiduguri near the Cameroon border, Gwoza is the administrative headquarters of the second-most-populous local government area (LGA) in Borno, and it has long been a target for Boko Haram and its predecessors. In late May, the emir of Gwoza, seventy-two-year-old Idrissa Timta, was killed in a roadside ambush while traveling to a funeral. Timta had been an outspoken critic of Boko Haram for years and had recently appealed to the Nigerian government for greater investment in the fight against them. On June 2, Boko Haram fighters dressed in Nigerian military uniforms staged raids against a number of small villages across the LGA, killing three hundred to five hundred civilians.

In retrospect, Gwoza's occupation marked the high-water mark for the insurgency. By now, Boko Haram fighters were consistently defeating Nigerian units in pitched battles. Residents were beginning to leave in large numbers, with as many as ten thousand from Gwoza alone fleeing over the state border to Adamawa and into Cameroon over the mountains. On August 24, a video of Shekau in Gwoza made its way into the hands of the local media. In what has now become one of his most famous appearances, he delivered a speech in front of three late-model SUVs with an AK-47 across his chest, while he read from what looks like a student's blue exam book. Declaring that "Allah has granted us success because we have risen to do [his] work," he proclaimed Gwoza the capital of a new Islamic state, to be ruled under shari'ah.[20] Over the next few months, Boko Haram extended this vision to its maximum, seizing a measure of control across a broad swath of territory covering nearly all of Borno (twenty or twenty-three LGAs, at its height) and into parts of Yobe and Adamawa and northern Cameroon. It also held a near stranglehold on the roads in and out of Maiduguri, and it was widely reported that its forces (including at least some artillery) planned an all-out assault in the near future.

How had Boko Haram gotten so strong? Obviously, its adaptability in the face of poor choices by the Nigerian military and government played an important role. While it does not seem to have been the group's first choice, the decision to become a rural insurgency in mid-2013 ultimately strengthened it considerably. In large part, this was because the countryside proved a fertile ground not only for challenging the military but also for "living off the land." Alongside revenue from the occasional kidnapping, the insurgents could now depend on violent raids that captured food, livestock, and other necessary goods for the group's sprawling camps and occupied communities. And perhaps even more important, it was able to leverage its financial resources amid the ruin it had created to secure the tacit or even outright support of local entrepreneurs, small-scale business operators, and farmers.

An interview project conducted in mid-2016 by the NGO Mercy Corps with former Boko Haram collaborators sheds some light on this issue. It found that Boko Haram offered to make cash investments in local informal businesses that no longer had customers, facilitate logistics for traders and animal herders stuck without easy access to markets, and even ensure access to inventory for shop owners. Occasionally these payments were used to recruit fighters, but more often they simply provided leverage that Boko Haram could use to obtain the resources it needed in its new territorial holdings—everything from achaba rides and consumer goods to a cut of long-distance trade revenues.[21]

But despite its economic savvy, Boko Haram made relatively little effort to govern its newfound state or to win over a majority of local hearts and minds. Videos released by the group in late 2014, for example, show group members receiving sermons from Shekau and highlight their military equipment but provide no evidence of public services. Indeed, the only real evidence of any community-facing efforts by the group during this time are reports of forcible conversion, mandatory Islamic instruction, and the execution of elderly locals unable to flee occupied territory. Not surprisingly, the result was that hundreds of thousands of local residents fled the area, finding shelter in IDP and refugee camps or (for the more lucky) with family across the country.

Why did Boko Haram not make more efforts to set up a state to govern the territories it had conquered? One reason was likely the sheer size. The territory in question, at roughly 30,000 square kilometers, was described in many international media reports as "the size of Belgium," but such a breathless comparison overstates the degree to which Boko Haram actually occupied it. Clustered in a handful of towns, camps, and along key routes in and out, the group's roughly seven thousand to ten thousand fighters successfully defended its territory against repeated incursions by Nigerian forces but were unable (as reports from escapees suggest) to garrison and govern the dozens of tiny rural villages under their sway. The significant divisions within the occupying force were another factor. Fulan Nasrullah, a Nigerian security analyst, has argued that even in late 2014, different factions were

Figure 2. "Wanted poster" showing Boko Haram's suspected leadership in mid-2015

holding various towns and surrounding areas without any real coordination with each other and in some cases even in direct opposition.[22]

Most important, however, was Shekau's own ideology of takfir and support of violence. In July 2014, Shekau recorded a video praising ISIS and expressing support for its leader, Abu Bakr al-Baghdadi. Soon after, the group's videos began reflecting some of ISIS's visual symbols and styles, a fact that led some analysts to argue that the links between the two were more than superficial. Yet, as we now know following ISIS's 2016 disavowal of Shekau, the relationship between the two groups was always uneasy. Factions within the movement seem to have wanted to affiliate with ISIS not only for the potential of material support but also to moderate Shekau, whose willingness to engage in violence against civilians would not have been (and, indeed, was not) acceptable to ISIS's leadership. It was not until the Nigerian military—this time, with help from regional allies—began to pry back its losses that the true devastation of Boko Haram's "Islamic state" was revealed.

A Tale of Two Countries

Although Boko Haram's violence was remaking northeastern Nigeria by early 2014, the conflict remained a more distant concern for many of Nigeria's political elite. On April 15, 2014, just as the information about the Chibok abductions was first becoming public and less than twenty-four hours after a bombing in Abuja, President Jonathan traveled to Kano to participate in a political rally. Ironically, the rally's goal was to show off his new alliances with influential Muslim politicians across the north in advance of the upcoming election cycle. While he appeared onstage dancing alongside former Kano governor Ibrahim Shekarau and prominent local Muslim film stars, the Nigerian Army announced that it had already launched a successful mission to rescue the girls and that the crisis was over. Within days, it was forced to admit that this had been an exaggeration; a few girls had escaped on their own, but the bulk remained missing. Meanwhile, not a single high-ranking administration official offered public comment, perhaps because the abductions undermined the official narrative that the government was winning the war against the militants. This sense of embarrassment, per-haps more than anything else, seems to have shaped the administration's next steps.

Remarkably, President Jonathan made no pub-lic statement about the events at Chibok at all until a "presidential media chat" on May 4, nearly three weeks later. In the meantime, Nigerians took matters into their own hands. One key moment was a speech on April 23 by Oby Ezekwezili, a former federal min-ister and World Bank vice president. Speaking at a UNESCO event in Port Harcourt, Ezekwezili called for Nigerians to "bring back all our daughters," an appeal that was transformed by an Abuja-based lawyer named Ibrahim M. Abdullahi into a pair of Twitter hashtags, #BringBackOurDaughters and #BringBackOurGirls. By the end of the month, the nascent movement had morphed into a series of nationwide protests, including a march on the National House of Assembly in Abuja that included some of the parents of the Chibok girls. The story had also become a regular headline in inter-national news. On May 2, the president put together an information-seeking committee.

On Sunday May 4, First Lady Patience Jonathan, who had first announced plans to join the marches, in-vited Borno officials and their wives, the principal of the Chibok school, and parents of the abducted girls to a meeting. Although it had been originally billed as a listening session, she instead preached at the attend-ees, scolded the principal, and wept theatrically in grief for the girls, often breaking into pidgin English, loudly and repeatedly proclaiming, "There is God-o." She also reproached protesters for allegedly plotting to embarrass and frame her husband. She accused the Abuja-based protest leader Naomi Mutah, representing the Chibok Women Development Association of Maiduguri at the meeting, of pretending to be a mother of one of the missing girls and called for her arrest. She ended the meeting at three o'clock in the morning, apparently convinced that the entire kidnapping was a hoax: "We the Nigerian women are saying that no child is missing in Borno State. If any child is missing, let the governor go and look for them. There is nothing we can do again."[1]

Patience Jonathan's accusatory tone and conspiratorial message were repeated often by those close to the presidency in the coming days and months. In Jonathan's presidential media chat, he promised to find the girls but also claimed that the parents had not been cooperative in helping identify them. And that night after their meeting with the First Lady, Naomi Mutah and another representative of the Chibok community were detained at the Asokoro Police Station, despite the fact that the First Lady had no official authority to order an arrest.

If Patience Jonathan was indeed motivated primarily by her concerns over how the abductions made her husband look, these actions did little to help. Her own performance had been recorded and broadcast nationally, and it spawned dozens of parodies and merciless mocking by Nigeria's savvy social media community.

Multiple reports in the Nigerian media have claimed that a clip of her theatrical wailing had become the most-watched nonmusic YouTube video in Nigerian history. But while many Nigerians experienced it as yet another funny viral meme about an outspoken political figure with bad English, those closest to the traumas of Boko Haram took little comfort in the First Lady's embarrassment.

Rebranding a Nigeria Besieged by Boko Haram

One plausible reason for the Jonathan administration's stunning lack of sensitivity to the Chibok kidnappings was its recognition that the plight of the girls had overtaken the administration's political messaging. Less than a month after the kidnappings, Nigeria played host to the World Economic Forum, a meeting the administration had intended to use to highlight a remarkable new development. On April 6, 2014, the Nigerian National Bureau of Statistics had released a new report, the result of an effort to update the country's outdated measurements about the size and scale of its economy. The results of this "rebasing" were astonishing. Overnight the estimated size of the Nigerian economy had nearly doubled from approximately N42 trillion (approximately $270 billion) to roughly N80 trillion (approximately $510 billion), making it officially the largest economy in Africa.

Although the rebasing exercise had little impact on ordinary Nigerians, the Jonathan administration certainly meant to use it as the most recent in a long series of "rebranding exercises" intended to improve Nigeria's international reputation. Yet even under the best of circumstances, news that the Nigerian economy was now the largest in Africa presented both opportunities and challenges. Although it reinforced the notion that the country was an increasingly powerful and prominent member of the global economic community, it was painfully clear to many Nigerian voters that this growth had taken place with only minimal improvements in the lives of many citizens. In the wake of the Chibok kidnappings, this contradiction was clearly on the minds of most of the journalists sent to cover the forum.

Nonetheless, the government seemed almost surprised that its narrative of progress might not be the most interesting thing going on. When confronted by an ABC News reporter at the Abuja Hilton hotel where the forum was being held, finance minister Ngozi Okonjo-Iweala expressed her frustrations, stating that "this is the second largest ever World Economic Forum after Davos. They've never had this kind of turnout, so terror has lost."[2] Of course, this was hardly the first time the administration had given the impression it simply did not want to talk about Boko Haram. Only the year before, Jonathan had been interviewed by CNN's Christiane Amanpour at the previous World Economic Forum, where he had challenged the legitimacy of the US State Department's Boko Haram–inspired travel advisory and told her that "ordinary Nigerians on the streets" were quite happy with the state of electricity in the country.

In June, just a few months after the kidnappings, it came to light that the Nigerian government had spent $1.2 million on a contract with the American public relations firm Levick to change "the international and local media narrative" around the Chibok abduction and to drum up support for fighting terrorism.[3] Levick's campaign had included an op-ed by President Jonathan in the *Washington Post* titled "Nothing Is More Important than Bringing Home Nigeria's Missing Girls." In it, he argued, "My silence has been necessary to avoid compromising the details of our investigation. But let me state this unequivocally: My government and our security and intelligence services have spared no resources, have not stopped and will not stop until the girls are returned home and the thugs who took them are brought to justice."[4] At home, Jonathan was mocked and criticized for speaking through an American paper when he had not spoken directly to Nigerians. Soon after, it was reported that the Nigerian Office of the National Security Adviser had spent $3 million in 2013 on lobbying in the United States to try to convince the US government to donate military equipment and that the Nigerian embassy in Washington had spent $700,000 on a public relations firm of its own.

This pressure to maintain a positive image abroad continued when, in November 2014, over three hundred schoolchildren were taken captive by Boko Haram in Damasak, near the border with Niger, with reports that around one hundred other women and children were also taken at the same time. Once more, the government initially denied anything had happened, and a local government administrator told AFP, "We kept quiet on the kidnap out of fear of drawing the wrath of the government, which was already grappling with the embarrassment of the kidnap of the Chibok schoolgirls."[5] The Damasak kidnappings and the thousands of smaller-scale abductions never received the same international or local attention as Chibok.

CAN and the Politics of Religion

As the first president from the minority "south-south" zone, home to the oil-rich Niger Delta, President Jonathan's supporters often spoke of the Boko Haram crisis as part of a northern Muslim conspiracy to undermine his government. The leadership of CAN, originally formed in the 1970s to advocate for Christian interests as the second republic's constitution was crafted, was one of the most important purveyors of this rhetoric. As the public representative of "Christians" in the country, Pastor Ayo Oritsejafor, the head of the association from 2010 to 2016, often showed up at events to "bless" and support Jonathan, and vice versa. In 2012, when Oritsejafor received the gift of a private jet from his congregation during a church anniversary, Jonathan was prominently photographed helping Oritsejafor cut the celebratory cake. In 2014, this same jet was caught ferrying $9.3 million in cash for the purchase of arms in South Africa. Although Oritsejafor claimed that he had rented the jet out to a third party, the government admitted that the money had been meant to purchase weapons for a security agency.

Oritsejafor's statements on Boko Haram cast the group and the government's efforts to combat it in terms of a stark national political conflict between Christians and Muslims, north and south. Not only did he complain that Boko Haram militants were pampered in prison, but he also circulated a series of press releases and newspaper advertisements issuing veiled threats of retaliation against the Muslim community in Nigeria as a whole. In December 2011, following yet another round of Christmas Day attacks, CAN and Oritsejafor placed a newspaper ad implicating mainstream Islamic clerics for Boko Haram activities, stating, "If the Supreme Council for Islamic Affairs [a leading Muslim civil-society organization] does not take positive action towards resolving the threat to our security by its extremist sects, particularly the Hausa and Fulani Muslims of Northern Nigeria, we might be forced to review our Christian/Muslim Collaborative efforts towards peace building." In the same communiqué, Oritsejafor threatened that "the Christian community nationwide may be left with no other option than to respond appropriately if there are any further attacks on our members, Churches and properties."[6]

Such rhetoric clearly reinforced the long-standing tensions between Muslim and Christian communities in places such as Plateau State, where violence was already sadly common. For example, after a March 2012 bombing at the Jos headquarters church of a local Protestant denomination, the Church of Christ in Nations (COCIN), a parishioner was killed by local youth who misidentified him as one of the bombers, several motorcyclists were killed by a mob, and Muslim businesses and homes in the area were torched. Christian youth in Kaduna engaged in similar "reprisal" attacks after three church bombings in June 2012, attacking and killing Muslim motorists.

Although the majority of Boko Haram's victims are Muslims, Christians were legitimately fearful of being targeted. For decades, Christian minorities in northern Nigeria have faced discrimination, suppression, and occasional attacks, which were rarely covered in the national press but chronicled in church publications such as *Today's Challenge,* a magazine published by the Jos-based denomination Evangelical Church Winning All (ECWA). After the 2011 election, disgruntled Muslim youth burned dozens of churches in cities across the north in retaliation for their alleged support of the Jonathan campaign, while other northern Christians (including colleagues of the authors) received threats.

Boko Haram's position on violence against Christians was also well established. In Abubakar Shekau's first video as Boko Haram leader in July 2010, he stated, "We want to fight [Christians]. You should rise up with your weapons, because we want to break your cross. We want to demolish all the churches, throw aside the constitution, and bring the law of Islam [into force], or else we perish."[7] In addition to high-profile attacks on Jos, Abuja, Zaria, and Kano, hundreds of churches across rural swaths of the northeast were destroyed during Boko Haram's occupation. In 2015, the president of the EYN Church of the Brethren, one of the most popular churches across the northeast, announced that, by EYN records, over eight thousand EYN members had been killed by Boko Haram. By 2017, that number had gone up to over eleven thousand, and 70 percent of EYN churches (as well as their denominational headquarters and a church-run Bible college) in the states of Adamawa, Yobe, and Borno had been destroyed. Of the kidnapped Chibok girls, 178 were EYN members, and smaller-scale kidnappings victimized others in the region.[8]

Yet neither the conspiratorial accusations of Patience Jonathan nor Oritsejafor's grandstanding reflect the complexities of Christian life in northern Nigeria. For one, while northern Christians are often depicted by those outside the region as immigrants from southern ethnic communities, a large percentage are actually members of local minority groups that have resisted conversion to Islam for centuries, while others are even members of predominantly Muslim ethnicities such as the Hausa, the Fulani, and the Kanuri. These Christians tend to belong to local church communities such as ECWA, EYN, and COCIN with long independent roots in the region. They often have "Muslim" names such as Amina and Abubakar and generally speak, dress, and live very much like their Muslim neighbors, to the extent that they sometimes pass as Muslims in the workplace.

Because of their experiences living alongside Muslims, northern Christians can sometimes be powerful voices against the stereotypes and misrepresentations of the region proffered by Christians in the south. Yet their histories as minorities have also made many of them suspicious of the motivations of the northern Muslim elite. Some Christians, particularly in Jos and Kaduna where there have been years of sectarian conflicts, engage in rhetoric similar to Oritsejafor's, using the example of Boko Haram atrocities to demonize all Muslims. For example, *Today's Challenge* frequently features articles comparing the persecution of Christians by Muslims around the world with injustices in Nigeria. These narratives have played an important role in driving increased distrust across religious lines. Indeed, with the rise of Boko Haram, even Christians with Muslim family members sometimes express suspicion that their relatives have colluded with Boko Haram.

CAN's rhetoric and the anger of northern Christians played directly into the hands of Boko Haram, whose goals clearly included both driving a wedge between Christian and Muslim Nigerians and greater international attention. Indeed, even before their transformation into a large-scale violent insurgency, Boko

Haram had fed rhetorically on acts of violence against Muslims, with Mohammed Yusuf using violence between Christians and Muslims in Jos as an example of abuse against Muslims in his sermons. During the July 2009 uprising, there were reports that Boko Haram members burned churches, killed Christians, and attempted to force others to convert. Later, in a video released in January 2012 after the Christmas Day church attacks, Shekau defended the attacks as revenge for the 2011 Eid el-Fitr attack in Jos by Christian youths on Muslims, documented on video, when they actually burned and ate parts of the bodies.

Aggressive rhetoric from CAN's national leadership and other Christian activists also obscured peacemaking efforts involving other northern Nigerian members of CAN in cities such as Kaduna, Jos, and Kano, including offering a prayer ground for Muslims at CAN headquarters in Kaduna during Lent in 2012, as well as the mutual protections Muslims and Christians have often offered each other during political protests and outbreaks of violence. Leaders such as the Catholic bishop of Sokoto, Matthew Hassan Kukah, and Kaduna-based Baptist pastor and CAN representative Joseph Hayeb have long argued that ordinary Christians and Muslims have no problem with each other and that a corrupt political class is behind Nigeria's religious conflicts. This perspective seemed to be shared by columnist Leonard Karshima Shilgba, writing for *Today's Challenge* in March 2015, right before the presidential election:

We do not need a "Christian" to lead Nigeria at this
moment of national collapse, common insecurity,
discouragement, hopelessness, and growing poverty.
We need a leader that is firm in conviction, who will
fight for and defend the downtrodden. Nigerians
need a fighter at this time. Nigerians need a friend of
the poor, not a once poor who has now become the
defender of the oppressors and obscene rich, whose
conscience apparently has been seared. If a pastor
prays something like this: "God give us a Christian
president; an Islamist should not be our president
in Jesus name," he is revealing some blindness that
should be pitied. Nigerians must without restraint
break in smithereens the bludgeoning pestle of
religion and ethnicity.[9]

An Electoral Turning Point?

By mid-2014, it had become increasingly difficult for
even the Jonathan administration's strongest supporters to ignore the worsening situation across the
northeast. Unrest among federal troops in Maiduguri,
Boko Haram's aggressive seizure of territories, and the
increasingly disheartening reports of Nigerian military
units being defeated in pitched battles all contributed
to a mounting sense of urgency to take new and aggressive action. In March, just before the Chibok attack, the
national security adviser (NSA), Colonel Sambo Dasuki, announced the adoption of a new, "soft" approach
to the fight against Boko Haram. It was to include

recommendations and best practices from the international community, an emphasis on winning community hearts and minds in the northeast, new programs to deradicalize youth recruited into Boko Haram, and improved communication and transparency from the military and the federal government. It was also to be accompanied by new military initiatives, including the purchase of new weapon packages designed for counterinsurgency operations and efforts to improve the conditions of troops in the region.

While these efforts were motivated by realities on the ground, they were also part of a worrying national political calculation. Although most Nigerians remained isolated from the conflict and its violence, a poll released by Gallup in July 2014 found that 95 percent of Nigerians now regarded Boko Haram as a "major threat" to the country's security. Moreover, a solid majority (67 percent) expressed significant dissatisfaction with the administration's handling of the situation, answering that they believed not enough had been done. They also found that approval in the country's leadership had fallen from 65 percent in 2011 to only 27 percent and that confidence in the military had shrunk from 78 percent to 57 percent.[10]

Another pressing issue was the increasingly organized character of Jonathan's opposition. In 2011, an important part of Jonathan's electoral success came from the fact that his most important challenger, former military head of state and retired general Muhammadu

Buhari, lacked the support of a strong national political party. Buhari—who had also run unsuccessfully as an opposition candidate in 2003 and 2007—instead relied largely on his reputation as an austere and incorruptible former military officer and on his appeal to Muslim voters, a strategy that allowed him to sweep thirteen Muslim-majority states across the north but resulted in a 27-percentage-point drubbing at the national level. The violence that followed in northern cities accurately represented northern Muslim frustrations at Buhari's defeat but provided no clear political path for the sixty-eight-year-old three-time loser.

Beginning in 2013, however, Buhari and his supporters began to strike a new series of bargains that would eventually lead to the creation of the All Progressives Congress (APC), the party that would take down the PDP in 2015. Of particular importance was the support of former Lagos State governor Bola Tinubu, whose international reputation as a pro-economic-growth and good-governance leader belied his behind-the-scenes skills as a kingmaker within Nigeria's patronage politics system. He also brought a well-oiled political machine to bear in the country's populous southwestern region, where Buhari had made few inroads, and played a central role in the selection of Yemi Osinbajo, an ordained Pentecostal minister and former Lagos State attorney-general, as Buhari's running mate. Despite their religiously diverse presidential ticket, the APC's leadership also agreed to not engage in the PDP's practice of "zoning"—essentially a guarantee that major ethnic and regional communities would each receive a proportional share of the party's leadership positions. Although the move was a political liability, it allowed the party to sell itself as that rarest of things in Nigeria: an open meritocracy. Buoyed by PDP defectors who saw the new party as an opportunity to move up the political ladder, the APC began the 2015 election cycle poised as a real threat to Jonathan's chances.

The campaign between Jonathan and Buhari focused less on insecurity and terrorism than on economic issues, corruption, and the integrity of the electoral process itself. But when the two parties debated the Boko Haram crisis, they told radically different stories. For Jonathan, the focus was on the military side, with an emphasis on retaking territory and "defeating" the insurgency through decisive battlefield encounters. In January 2015, just days after a Boko Haram attack on the town of Baga that left two thousand civilians dead, Jonathan traveled to Maiduguri in order to emphasize his newfound awareness of the conflict's human toll and to promise a military victory. Yet with attacks in the news nearly every day, this was a difficult line to sell. His campaign also made a handful of political blunders. In September 2014, for example, supporters put up a billboard in Abuja with the slogan "#BringBackJonathan2015," which drew scathing reviews from the local and international press.

As the presidential election drew closer, members of the Jonathan administration became increasingly vocal in their accusations that the real reason behind the military's slow progress was the unwillingness of its international partners—particularly the Americans—to work with it on arms sales. Within some Nigerian political circles, this reluctance—partly driven by US legal requirements that military assistance not be provided to units with a record of gross human rights violations—was interpreted as favoritism toward Buhari. In late 2014, the Jonathan administration abruptly canceled a planned joint training exercise as a sign of its displeasure.

Buhari took advantage of the visibility of the Bring Back Our Girls protests to strike at the Jonathan administration's failure. His campaign played up not only his military background but also his reputation (particularly during the Maitatsine crisis) for "toughness" against violent armed groups. The APC was also not shy about pointing out that Sheriff's PDP administration in Borno State had cooperated with Yusuf and other early members of his movement during the 2003 election campaign. Perhaps most damning, however, were the APC's allegations that the Jonathan administration's mounting security spending (roughly 25 percent of the national budget by 2014) had become a political boondoggle for the benefit the president's political allies. After Buhari's victory, these accusations turned into the November 2015 arrest of (by then former) NSA Dasuki on allegations that his office had given out as many as $2 billion worth of phony military procurement contracts and facilitated nearly $150 million in unexplained and undocumented payments to contractors.

Another key turning point in the campaign was NSA Dasuki's proposal, announced in late January 2015, that the Nigerian Independent National Electoral Commission (INEC) postpone the elections, scheduled for mid-February. On its face, the request had merit. The INEC, under the direction of former university vice chancellor Attahiru Jega, had suffered from a series of missteps and delays in distributing its new voter-identification and registration cards. Combined with the security situation in Borno, the very real possibility of Boko Haram attacks, and the difficulty of ensuring access to the polls for residents who had fled their home communities, it certainly made sense to at least consider the option.

And yet the decision to delay was clearly political. Just days before the final announcement, Jega was informed that the military had begun a major offensive against Boko Haram, which meant troops would be unavailable to provide security during polling. Given the timing, it seems likely that the offensive was intended to provide the Jonathan administration with a positive story on the eve of the newly rescheduled elections, which were officially delayed until March 28 (federal, including presidential) and April 11 (state). Among international observers and some APC supporters in Nigeria, the postponement was also interpreted as an attempt to buy time until the polls could be sufficiently rigged to produce a PDP victory.

Over the next six weeks, the government's counteroffensive produced significant military gains. It also demonstrated the power of regional cooperation. Boko Haram had included Nigeria's Lake Chad basin neighbors in its strategic thinking going as far back as the original Hijra Group, whose members had fled across the Cameroon border when pursued by Nigerian forces. But since the group's transformation in 2010, it had slowly but surely ramped up its transborder attacks, eventually coming to pose nearly as large a security threat in the borderlands as it originally had in Maiduguri. Reports coming from these countries had long suggested reluctance on the Nigerian side to more closely integrate the regional war against terrorism. In principle, Nigeria and its neighbors cooperated via the Multi-National Joint Task Force (MNJTF), a joint military command originally created as a sort of border patrol in the late 1990s and officially given a counterterrorism remit in 2012. But in January 2015, the MNJTF's command in Baga had been overrun, and it was clear that without a new international commitment, it would be of little use. In February, following a meeting of the African Union's Peace and Security Council, that commitment was finally announced in the form of a proposed 8,500 troop deployment under the MNJTF's command and a new headquarters in the Chadian capital, N'djamena. Soon after, coordinated air strikes by Chadian and Nigerian forces cleared the way for ground troops from Cameroon, Chad, and Niger to surge into Borno alongside Nigerian forces.

The fight was not without controversy. Boko Haram staged a series of retaliatory suicide bombings, driving up civilian death counts and raising questions about whether or not these victories were actually diminishing the group's capabilities. And just the day before the election, the *New York Times* published a story based on interviews with Chadian president Idriss Deby, who alleged that Chadian forces had done most of the offensive's heavy military lifting. Moreover, he claimed that, in some cases, Chadian units that had routed Boko Haram forces inside Nigeria had been unable to make contact with their local military counterparts, who were (he alleged) unprepared for any handover of responsibility.[11] Despite these hiccups, Nigerian forces announced just days before the election that they were once more in possession of Boko Haram's "capital" at Gwoza.

Unfortunately for Jonathan, these gains came too late. Public polling data (and, allegedly, some internal PDP reports) had long suggested that the election would be too close to call if conducted fairly, and when voting finally opened on March 28, it quickly became clear that another PDP rout was not forthcoming. Following a remarkably violence-free polling exercise, millions of Nigerians watched on television as Jega and the INEC staff collated and tallied state voting results on March 31, an effort that, it was later revealed, was nearly sabotaged by PDP supporters from the Niger Delta region who planned to disrupt the proceedings and throw the results into question. Despite significantly lower turnout than in 2011, Buhari was able to eke out a 53 percent national majority, carrying twenty-one states (including Tinubu's southwestern bloc) to Jonathan's fifteen.

The APC's victory was one of the most iconic moments in West African political history, but it left unanswered important questions about the future of the war against Boko Haram. While the troop surge and increased regional military cooperation had both helped degrade Boko Haram's capacity to hold and occupy territory, it had not been routed. Reports indicated that just as they had before, fighters were already regrouping in camps along the borderlands and in the Sambisa Forest. Meanwhile, optimism at home and abroad that Buhari's election would usher in a new era of reform and a speedy end to corruption in the security sector badly underestimated the challenges a new administration would face in actually carrying them out. By the end of 2015, the honeymoon was over.

Conspiracy Theories

Following Buhari's victory, conspiracy theories about Boko Haram's true motives and connections to political power gained new traction, aided by the viral nature of social media. Dismissing testimony given by eyewitnesses, a growing number of skeptics began to claim that the Chibok kidnapping had been a hoax intended to help the APC. Nor were many of those giving voice to these accusations merely Internet "trolls" on the fringe. Even some influential members of the literary community, most based outside of the country or in southern regions far from the conflict, were involved in what they called "asking questions" about the Chibok abduction.

The pattern this "questioning" took is similar to that employed by conspiracy theorists in the United States and other Western countries. Skeptics took relatively minor (and easily explainable) questions about how the kidnappings were conducted and presented them as evidence of its fundamental implausibility, asking, for example, how so many teenage girls could have been captured without the girls calling or texting their parents to let them know what was happening. Not surprisingly, as more firsthand information emerged from the girls themselves, this claim simply proved false. Other voices simply accused the girls and their families of lying (or being paid off by unidentified sources) or drew on stereotypes about the region to suggest that the girls were never even at school in the first place. One popular rumor suggested that given the relatively low number of young women in school across the northeast in the first place, it was unbelievable that there were two hundred girls studying physics (and not, say, religious studies) in Chibok. At their worst, they simply dismissed the kidnapping out of hand, playing on the number of girls kidnapped to joke that "419" of them had been kidnapped, a play on the term commonly used to describe the Nigeria's legendary Internet fraudsters (419 being the applicable section of the Nigerian Criminal Code).

Nor did the eventual escape or release of many of the abductees silence these skeptics. On social media, conspiracy theorists pored over photos of the girls taken during their brief public appearances, claiming that they looked too well fed to have been in Boko Haram's clutches. And after the numbers of returnees mounted, many simply pivoted away from denying the abductions had never taken place and toward claims that it had been a political setup (with sponsored kidnappers) to bring Buhari to power.

Conspiracy theories have a long history in Nigeria and are encouraged by the secretive machinations of Nigeria's political elite, who often operate with such audacity that some of the more outrageous accusations against them occasionally turn out to be true. As the anthropologist Karin Barber once noted, the rapid influx of oil money into the country in the 1970s created a new class of superwealthy Nigerians, nearly all of whom owed their new status to their participation in shady dealings that were poorly understood by most ordinary citizens. The sudden appearance of these wealthy, politically connected elites, with their new houses, international travel, and flashy appearances, not only challenged long-standing social norms of morality and social reciprocity but also created a sort of cottage industry of speculation about how and why these particular Nigerians had come to be so fantastically rich.[12]

The stories that emerged in news reports—complex schemes to double-bill the Nigerian government for oil deliveries, disguise the true owners of petroleum-extraction contracts, and hide the resulting wealth—

sometimes exceeded even the most far-fetched theories circulating on the street. For their part, the Nigerian media often revel in these stories, particularly those with a hint of the occult. Newspapers often publish stories about politicians and other wealthy people caught in ritual attempts to use sorcery to gain wealth, while Nigeria's film industries have long thrived on bringing rumors, urban legends, and stories ripped from newspaper headlines to the screen, often attributing the wealth of Nigeria's governing class to moral corruption and membership in occult secret societies.

Nigeria's history of corruption also means that Nigerians are often (rightly) skeptical about the motivations of international actors. In the north, polio vaccines were thought to be a conspiracy by Western powers to sterilize Muslims—suspicions furthered by a 1996 pharmaceutical trial for meningitis organized by the international drug company Pfizer in Kano, in which eleven children died. In the north, resentment and distrust of Western governments and economic interests also often coincides with anti-Semitic conspiracy theories or global speculation about the mythical Illuminati. The anti-Semitic forgery *The Protocols of the Elders of Zion* is readily available at small bookshops and at traffic stops in the north. Opinion columns in the north's largest paper, the *Daily Trust*, occasionally peddle familiar conspiracy theories, including Holocaust denial and claims that the attack on the World Trade Center was an inside job. And in both southern Nigeria and Nigeria's populous (and heavily Christian-majority) diaspora, long-standing resentments and prejudices against northern politicians make it easier to accept claims that require imagining that hundreds of people are lying on their behalf. Social media platforms such as Facebook, Twitter, and WhatsApp ensure that these stories spread more rapidly than ever before. On social media, however, the loudest voices of commentary on conflict in the north have often been those with the most access to the Internet and smartphones and many times those living the farthest from the region.

Conspiracy thinking about Boko Haram also builds on the reality that in the early 2000s ambitious northern politicians did in fact strike shadowy deals with Yusuf and his allies to exchange their support for money and recognition. And because the military has often failed people living in areas prone to attack, it is easy to understand why even some of the families with kidnapped daughters would accuse school administrators of complicity, asking why the vice principal had insisted that the girls stay in the school overnight or circulating rumors that none of the children of the teachers had been taken. The lack of answers from the government about the military's failures only deepens this distrust.

Bringing Back "Our" Girls

In May 2016, the first Chibok abductee to emerge from the Sambisa Forest since shortly after the original kidnapping was introduced to the public. After two years of

151

captivity, she was found by a civilian vigilante, carrying her four-month-old daughter and saying that she had escaped Boko Haram. To the Buhari administration, her "rescue" was a coup in the ongoing war, not only against the group but also against its domestic and international critics who claimed that despite more than a year in office, the administration had not yet come close to defeating Boko Haram. In the days following her return, she was shuttled through photo ops with President Buhari and military medical personnel who leaned solicitously down over her baby, a visible symbol of the government's success in "bringing back the girls."

The reality was more complex. Along with her baby, she had escaped with a man she called her husband but whom the government alleged was a known insurgent. Following her appearance in Abuja, she and the child were taken to a safe house, while her husband was remanded for "rehabilitation" in a government-run deradicalization center. The former abductee's mother returned to Chibok shortly after the rescue and, when interviewed in August, reported that she had not had access to either her daughter or granddaughter in months.

Both the administration's efforts to score political points with this story and much of the public response to it had little to say about the complexities of this young woman's story. On Facebook and Twitter, for example, many Nigerians condemned the local press's choice to refer to her child's father as her "husband," when in fact (as they saw it) he was little more than a rapist.

Interviews with other returnees and escapees from Boko Haram camps, however, have pointed out just how complicated the choices made and relationships forged under such circumstances could be. Indeed, the young woman's family defended him after a fashion, stating that he himself had been forced into Boko Haram's service when his own community had been attacked. And for her part, the young woman spoke openly in interviews about how she missed him and the difficulty of her life in the safe house without him.

This pattern, in which Boko Haram's most notorious victims were forced uneasily into the public eye with little regard to their own needs for privacy and the ability to tell their own stories their own way, would soon reoccur on a much larger scale. In October 2016, following a series of clandestine negotiations, a group of twenty-one Chibok abductees was released to the government. And seven months later, in May 2017, another group of eighty-two was freed, this time in exchange for at least five captured Boko Haram commanders (and, as it came out later, a multi-million-euro ransom). Again, the administration rushed the young women into hastily arranged presidential photo ops before they were allowed to see their families, and again they were held in Abuja (ostensibly for "psychological debriefing") with no specific timetable for their return. Critics complained that the government was keeping the girls under closer watch than Boko Haram members, while family members spoke of hours-long waits to see them when the twenty-one released in October were allowed (briefly) to return to Chibok during the Christmas season.

Not surprisingly, some family members expressed relief at these arrangements, noting that at least the girls were safe. For their part, government officials protested that the high security location of the girls was for their protection and released videos of well-dressed girls in the classroom speaking about how happy they were about being able to continue their educations. Besides physical security, the celebrity of the Chibok girls also provided them opportunities not afforded to most other victims of the group. In many cases, the most high-profile returnees were effectively "adopted" by prominent politicians, provided special housing, and given preferential treatment by the government, as well as offered scholarships by NGOs and American million-aires to study in elite schools in Nigeria and the United States. It was as if by providing for the most famous of the lost young people of the northeast, Nigeria's political elite could assuage their responsibility for the millions of other displaced people. At the same time, as novelist Adaobi Tricia Nwaubani put it, the girls were often "prisoners of fame." Those brought to the United States were taken on speaking tours, expected to tell their stories over and over again, and often treated as representatives of abducted women as a whole. One of the fathers of the girls expressed concerned that "they are being used for show business.... That is not what we wanted for our children."[13]

In a December 2015 interview with the British Broadcasting Corporation (BBC), President Buhari stated that government forces had "technically" won the war against Boko Haram. He went on to explain that with much of the group's territory reclaimed and their military strength "reduced" to improvised-explosive-device and suicide attacks, there was little to prevent people from returning to their homes, farms, and lives.[14] But while it was true enough that the military situation had improved, this claim of victory rang hollow with many if not most Nigerians. Certainly, the year following the Chibok abductions, the Bring Back Our Girls demonstrations, and Buhari's own historic victory had made far more Nigerians aware of the conflict and its consequences than ever before. But what had not changed was the distance between the voices that were heard the loudest and those that were most affected. If anything, the year that brought the war home to most Nigerians had once more replicated the tale of "two Nigerias": those who experienced the conflict through the political struggle between the PDP and the APC, in the press (domestic and international), and online, and those who, even with occasional opportunities to tell their stories to the cameras, still had little say in what would come next. Beyond the headlines and the discussion spaces dominated by a cosmopolitan elite, however, there were other conversations happening that deserve hearing. It is to these voices that we now turn.

Who Speaks for Boko Haram's Victims?

In her 1988 essay "Can the Subaltern Speak?" the Indian postcolonial scholar Gayatri Spivak argues that often even the best-intentioned outsiders who attempt to bring the struggles of poor, marginalized, and victimized peoples to a broader audience inadvertently reinforce many of the very problems they set out to solve. Although they may amplify and empower the voices of people who rarely have access to the world stage, she argues, the cost is a loss of complexity, of the diversity of these "subaltern" communities that come to be defined by how privileged people speak about their struggle.

Spivak's concerns are important for how Western audiences talk about and access information about Boko Haram and those it affects. Although efforts such as the global Bring Back Our Girls movement brought attention to the conflict and raised important points about how the Western media prioritizes the victims of certain sorts of violence over others, the picture of the conflict available to outsiders imperfectly captures the diversity of responses offered by Nigerians who experience it every day. And even though Western media reporting has often provided detailed, nuanced, and genuinely moving accounts of the conflict and its victims, the full scope of the experiences of those who face the fear of Boko Haram every day remains elusive. There is much to learn from the way Nigerians themselves speak to the Boko Haram crisis, often in ways that point to a deep longing for a peaceful multireligious and multiethnic society.

The Problem of the Media

In May 2017, a self-styled "free lance journalist" named "Odera N. O." briefly became something of a celebrity in Nigerian social media circles when she claimed that she had gone to Chibok several years earlier and had learned from people she spoke to there that the abduction of the Chibok girls was a political conspiracy. When challenged on her version of events on Twitter, she wrote, "You have your Chibok experience I have mine. Don't distort MY truth!" Social media had democratized access to information, but it had also enabled conspiracy theories and opinions to not only look like real investigative journalism but have some of its power as well, an issue that has become a global problem in the past decade.

Part of the problem starts at home. Although they have a long and independent history of muckraking and confronting power, Nigerian journalistic institutions also face profound economic and structural challenges in their quest to cover the news. Most Nigerian newspapers and media houses lack the resources to promote investigative journalism or to train their reporters to be successful at it, with the result that local reporters are often forced to rely on official statements, press releases, and other government-sponsored narratives to do their work. And while some Nigerian reporters and editors have famously stood up to power (Dele Giwa, the courageous editor and founder of *Newswatch* magazine, for example, was assassinated in 1986 as part of a government plot that included then military head of state General Ibrahim Babangida), most media houses today are known as being poorly paying employers in the pockets of wealthy donors who often pay for coverage.

Not surprisingly then, Nigerians regularly look to outside news agencies to verify information about current events at home. As Achebe slyly observed in *Anthills of the Savannah,* the morning routine for the Minister for Information included listening to the BBC for news about his country. Thirty years later, millions of Nigerians, particularly those in the north, still listen religiously to the BBC, the Voice of America, Radio Deutsche Welle, China Radio International, and other foreign news services broadcast daily in Hausa. Nigerian newspapers regularly reprint articles that first appeared in foreign media outlets and rely on the work done by reporters working for global press agencies for stories. In a 2014 editorial for the popular Nigerian newspaper *Vanguard* titled "Chibok and the Failure of Reporting," the prominent journalist Lanre Idowu excoriated the state of the Nigerian press:

From the owners to the reporters, everyone is sworn to a journalism of convenience. This mindset explains why no medium invests enough resources to report stories beyond the relative comfort of urban centres, much less one in a conflict zone. . . . It took CNN's visit to Chibok for Nigerians to get a guided visual tour of the burnt school and comprehend the enormity of the damage. It is also from CNN that we had glimpse of a victim's account of her ordeal on television. It is also from them that hard probing questions on the Nigerian experience, which should be the hallmark of reporting, resurfaced on television as our Information minister was forced to shift gear from his usual self-assured soapbox-like exhortations to mumbling excuses for inaction.[1]

While Idowu's article expresses the frustrations of Nigerians with their media, there was real diversity in how local reporters and outlets actually covered the conflict. Newspapers based in the north such as the *Daily Trust, Blueprint,* and *Leadership* and their Hausa-language counterparts were closer to events and typically employed more reporters with local language skills. Their coverage was often more detailed and comprehensive than that of media companies based outside the region. Journalist and former *Daily Trust* editor Abdullahi Tasiu Abubakar has described how, for a few months in 2012, journalists from northern-based papers and stringers for international news agencies based in Maiduguri were able to access information from Boko Haram via "news conferences" over mobile phones using undisclosed numbers, while others without staff on the ground were excluded.[2] And even in July 2018, four years after the abductions, the *Daily Trust* continued to print on its masthead the number of days since the Chibok girls had been taken—the only Nigerian newspaper to make such a visible commitment to following up on the issue.

The best journalism on Boko Haram and its aftermath tended to come from those who know northern Nigeria well but had the resources of wealthier institutions behind them. In Helon Habila's sensitive and carefully researched 2016 book *The Chibok Girls: The Boko Haram Kidnappings and Islamist Militancy in Nigeria*, he interviews people in Chibok, including some of the girls who first escaped from Boko Haram. His knowledge of Hausa and his familiarity with the region—he grew up in Gombe in northeastern Nigeria—meant that he was able to access firsthand information that Western journalists often misunderstood or oversimplified, and he carefully protected his sources by changing or using incomplete names. Author and journalist Abubakar Adam Ibrahim published award-winning journalism about people living in IDP camps for *Granta*, while continuing to write for *Daily Trust*, where he was an editor. And Andrew Walker's *"Eat the Heart of the Infidel": The Harrowing of Nigeria and the Rise of Boko Haram*, also published in 2016 and based on years of reporting in northern Nigeria for the BBC, gives a historical context for the conflict and has received much critical acclaim from Nigerian readers who know the context.

For their part, international media houses had more resources than local papers to cover the conflict and were sometimes given appointments for interviews more quickly by government and military officials. But these advantages did not always translate into better or more ethical coverage. This was particularly true in the immediate aftermath of the Chibok abductions, when the international media often gained the first access to information about the girls (including their names) and their parents. In particular, CNN and other international entities quickly displayed photos of the missing girls on air and broadcast interviews with their parents identified by name. This coverage provided important insight into the abductions (and the government's inaction) and helped encourage the growth of online activism, but it did little to reckon with the challenges of covering a group with a history of retaliating against its perceived enemies. Boko Haram attacked Chibok again in June 2014, and by November the community was briefly occupied, effectively placing at risk all of those who had spoken on camera.

News outlets in the United States and Europe were often surprisingly cavalier about coverage that identified Boko Haram's victims, often in ways that were unlikely to have been consented to freely and openly. In many cases, girls' names and photos were embedded in stories that seemed intended to titillate or scandalize, with headlines such as "214 Girls Kidnapped by Boko Haram are Free Now—and Pregnant"[3] or "Nigeria: Boko Haram Impregnated Girls 'to Guarantee New Generation of Fighters.'"[4] Such stories played up the sexual violence suffered by victims in order to drum up readership. Sensational headlines and the photographs of identifiable women used to illustrate them further contributed to the stigma that women returning from Boko Haram camps faced.

Nor was this trend restricted to tabloid-style reporting. One of the most egregious was the photograph in the United Kingdom's *Sunday Times* of a young girl gazing pensively into the camera, captioned with her full name and the information that she "was only 11½ when she was captured by Boko Haram. She is now 13 and pregnant by a terrorist. She escaped in January, and is in a refugee camp."[5] In an article critiquing the lack of sustained international attention to the crisis as well as the stigma attached to female victims of sexual violence in conflict zones, neither the journalist, the photographer, nor the editor seemed to have any qualms about publishing the full name or photograph of a thirteen-year-old rape victim alongside her detailed testimony of what she had experienced.

Such questionable practices raise important questions about the standards used by Western journalists in Africa covering stories about violence and conflict. In 2010, popular *New York Times* columnist Nicolas Kristof faced outrage for his choice to identify a nine-year-old rape victim from the Democratic Republic of Congo in one of his columns. Responding to the uproar, Kristof argued that that "it's impossible to get rape on the agenda when the victims are anonymous. Human beings just aren't hard-wired to feel compassion for classes of victims, but for individuals."[6] In similar terms, Lynsey Addario, an American photojournalist who took the photograph of a nearly naked pregnant rape survivor from Sudan that became the cover of *Time* magazine in March 2016, has argued that she had gained informed consent from the woman photographed and that, indeed, being named and photographed was empowering for survivors of rape.[7]

These explanations about empowerment and activism may be true in some instances, but they fail to fully grapple with the broader circumstances under which such stories are written. Language barriers, power differentials, and a lack of awareness of the potential reach of such media exposure all complicate the ability of Western journalists to obtain real consent from victims of groups such as Boko Haram. Indeed, a photojournalist working in Nigerian IDP camps told one of the authors that permission had to be sought from the camp and from the individual, yet the widespread abuse in the camps calls into question whether the consent of a subject is necessarily made freely.

One counterargument advanced by Kristof is that in places like the Congo (or, presumably, Nigeria), a lack of access to global media helps protect from potential retribution those whose names and faces are exposed.

As he argued, the young girl he had named lived in a community where no one "ever sees any newspaper or the Internet. . . . The people there speak no English and minimal French. In short, it seems to me that there's zero chance that the column or video is going to reach these communities in which these women live or haunt them in any way." Seven years later, the Internet is much more accessible all over Africa, with over 50 percent of Nigerians able to access it via their mobile devices. Indeed, Boko Haram makes regular use of the Internet in uploading its videos, and videos and photos produced by the group regularly circulate via Bluetooth and WhatsApp. In other words, photographs and stories ostensibly "meant" for Western audiences are almost as easily accessible in regions where victims are at risk of attack and stigma.

The question of how international coverage of Boko Haram's victims might contribute to their local stigmatization or reprisals by Boko Haram is rarely explored. Although the Chibok girls who first escaped from Boko Haram or the women in the IDP camps may have consented to having their photographs taken in a public setting, they had no way of knowing that their photographs would be paired with headlines about sexual violence. Given the care taken by human rights activists such as Human Rights Watch, Amnesty International, and the International Crisis Group, it remains puzzling why the *Sunday Times* and other outlets fail to adopt policies such as mandatory pseudonyms for the victims of terrorist groups and sexual violence in the Global South. Yet as recently as April 2018, the *New York Times* published a series of eighty-three named portraits of returned Chibok girls and identified where the government is housing them, noting that they "are not allowed to leave . . . without an escort."[8] The author of the piece relates how frustrating it was to be refused "permission to photograph the ex-captives" until finally, "after weeks of persuasion," they were allowed to photograph those who consented.[9] Yet, as with the journalists who photographed women in refugee camps, there seemed to be little thoughtfulness about how they might be exploiting or even endangering these young women, who even after their release from Boko Haram had very little choice in what they did with their lives.

Yet it would not be fair to blame international journalists alone. The Nigerian government also distributed photographs of the abductees, and when the Chibok girls began to return, it regularly exposed them and their babies to cameras at public events, even as it justified their seclusion and restricted access to their families on security grounds. Notably, some Nigerian publications based in the north were more sensitive about showing faces and names. In the July 1, 2014, issue of the ECWA magazine *Today's Challenge,* the story "Chibok: An Untold Story of Kidnap of Christian Teenagers" was illustrated with photographs of six of the missing girls with their faces blacked out. But many Nigerian media houses widely distributed, alongside sensational headlines, photos of women who had just come back from camps.

Even activists sometimes did not take care to protect these women's privacy. Emmanuel Ogebe, an attorney who arranged for several of the escaped Chibok abductees to come to the United States to complete their education, nonetheless regularly took them out of school for media appearances. The former abductee who testified before the US Congress took a pseudonym to protect her identity, and *Time* magazine recounted how the girls told their school director that "they didn't want to be videotaped nor be interviewed because they were told their families would be put in danger." Yet in media interviews arranged by Ogebe, they were often only given sunglasses to protect their identities.

Writing Africa, Writing Boko Haram

For decades before the Boko Haram crisis, African writers have been pushing back at sensationalistic and dehumanizing images of the continent. Chinua Achebe said in 1965 that he would be satisfied if his novel *Things Fall Apart* "did no more than teach my readers that their past—with all its imperfections—was not one long night of savagery from which the first Europeans acting on God's behalf delivered them."[10] In 2005, Kenyan author Binyavanga Wainaina wrote a satirical essay, "How to Write about Africa," that skewered media coverage of the continent. For example: "Among your characters you must always include The Starving African, who wanders the refugee camp nearly naked and waits for the benevolence of the West. Her children have flies on their eyelids and pot bellies and her breasts are flat and empty. She must look utterly helpless. She can have no past, no history; such diversions ruin the dramatic moment."[11]

At issue for both of these writers were degrading images promoted by foreigners that contributed to stereotypes about Africa and often served an ulterior motive to excuse exploitation. Wainaina explained that he was responding to *Granta*'s "Africa" issue, "which was populated by every literary bogeyman that any African has ever known. . . . It wasn't the grimness that got to me, it was the stupidity. There was nothing new, no insight, but lots of 'reportage' . . . as if Africa and Africans were not part of the conversation."[12]

Nigerian author Chimamanda Ngozi Adichie built on these critiques in her 2009 TED talk "The Danger of a Single Story," where she spoke about how media images can overpower individual human stories. She pointed out the importance of looking at multiple stories of a place or people rather than lazily relying on stereotypes. By the 2010s, however, other critics began to build on this long-standing concern of African intellectuals about the way foreign writers represented Africa, to attack African writers who delved into grim topics as well.

But what about African writers and artists who wanted to tackle the very real violence and conflict in their societies? Those who gain international exposure face accusations of catering to the sensationalist desires of Western readers to see poverty and suffering in Africa—of producing what is sometimes called "poverty porn," a term first developed as a critique of Western charity campaigns that exploited voyeuristic images of the poor to raise money. Shortly before Boko Haram began to garner international attention, US-based Nigerian critic and social media influencer Ikhide R. Ikheloa critiqued the short list for the 2011 UK-based Caine Prize for African Writing: "Aided by some needy 'African' writers, Africa is being portrayed as an issues-laden continent that is best viewed on a fly-infested canvas."[13] While this frustration was understandable in the context of a decades-old literary tradition of pushing back at misrepresentations of Africa, the problem of applying the concept of poverty porn to African writers resident in Africa is that it often becomes a way to judge stories simply by their topic, even if the actual content is careful and nuanced.

At the 2013 Africa Writes event in London, a judge of the previous year's Caine Prize contest, Bernadine Evaristo, told an audience how, during her time as chair of the prize committee, she "was absolutely determined that we were not going to have any traumatized children winning this prize." She described her "battle" to make sure one story "which ticked all the boxes . . . a boy living in a terrible situation, prey to gangs, brutalized etc." did not win the prize. Ironically, this declaration in

London came on the same day that forty-two school-boys and their teachers in Mamudo, Yobe State, were slaughtered in their beds by Boko Haram. Attempts, particularly by writers and cultural critics living abroad, to discourage literary voices living on the continent from writing about suffering characters seemed to prioritize the voices of the privileged over the voices of those living amid crisis. In a time when Boko Haram had also threatened local journalists and bombed the newspaper *This Day* in April 2012, it seemed that writers writing about environments they knew well were being threatened by violence within Nigeria and by shaming on the outside.

For northern Nigerian writers, this issue was particularly poignant. On the one hand, they were frustrated with sensationalistic coverage of the north coming both from the international press and from southern Nigerian cultural producers. Often northern intellectuals directed their writing and creative productions at southern audiences in an attempt to challenge stereotypes. In September 2011, Maiduguri-based blogger Mark Amaza wrote a widely circulated essay, "Re-Introducing Northern Nigeria: Not as You Know It," in which he took on the myths "held by most Southerners about the North." Building on Adichie's TED talk "The Danger of the Single Story," Amaza wrote about the danger of the "single story of the North as a region of poor, illiterate, lazy, Hausa Muslims who do nothing but connive to lord over this country politically and kill Southerners."[14]

On the other hand, writers and other artists based in the north also recognized the need to capture the stories of both ordinary lives and the extraordinary times. In 2012, a year after his article written in frustration at misconceptions of the north, Amaza wrote a melancholy piece about losing a friend to Boko Haram, "Living under Siege in Maiduguri":

> Curfews of 7pm have eliminated all nightlife; people go out only if they have to; large crowds are avoided and there is an air of insecurity that hangs permanently over the city. Parents no longer long for their children to come home to visit, while checkpoints have made traffic hellish. Church services have numerously been ended suddenly mid-way, while a tradition of hospitality has died as suspicion towards unknown people is very high. Young children are growing up getting used to the sign of guns and the sound of gunfire. This isn't life.[15]

Similarly, Elnathan John, a columnist, lawyer, and novelist, wrote in a conversation with other African writers on Facebook in 2012 in response to conversations about poverty porn in African literature:

> Where I live, EVERYTHING is driven by fear of conflict, bomb blasts, and daylight assassinations unreported by the media. Every kilometer of road has a checkpoint like those in the Occupied Palestinian Territories. Now, I am a writer writing my realities.... Our problems in Africa will not disappear when we stop writing about them.[16]

In 2013, John was nominated for the Caine Prize for his story "Bayan Layi." He expanded the story into the novel *Born on a Tuesday*, which imagines a Boko Haram–like insurgency in the northwest. John emphasizes in interviews that while he has written about Boko Haram in nonfiction and other short stories, *Born on a Tuesday* is not about Boko Haram. Rather, it tells stories about what could happen with similar movements, from a perspective of the most often maligned people of the north, the young almajirai.

In *Born on a Tuesday*, an almajiri named Dantala is caught up in violence in a town where he has gone to study before returning to his northwestern home state of Sokoto. In Sokoto, he is taken in by a kind imam, Sheikh Jamal, who gives him a place to stay in the mosque. Here, Dantala observes both the mosque's growing political influence and the conflict between the sheikh and his increasingly extremist deputy, Malam Abdul-Nur. Abdul-Nur eventually separates from his mentor to found a jihadist group, which moves to a rural area where it begins military-style training. Dantala, who has learned much about Islam, love, and the world surrounding him in the years with Sheikh Jamal, is eventually caught between the violence of the extremists and the brutal government response.

In interviews, John has pointed to the parallels between Sheikh Jamal's relationship with Malam Abdul-Nur and the debates between Ja'afar Adam and Mohammed Yusuf in the mid-2000s.[17] There are also parallels between the 2003 withdrawal of the Hijra Group to Kanama and the fictional "hijra" of Malam Abdul-Nur's extremist group. And there are certainly similarities between the violent government retaliation against the group in the novel and the government's retaliation against Boko Haram, in which both innocent and guilty were detained in inhumane prison conditions and even executed without trial.

However, by insisting that the novel is not about Boko Haram, John also targets the dysfunction of northern Nigerian society in which other previous religious dissenters have emerged and faced the cycle of government violence. As John and others have noted, this cycle has not yet ended, as, in the years since the 2009 Boko Haram uprising, members of the minority Shi'a Muslim community in northern Nigeria have faced an escalating pattern of harassment, arrest, and violence from the state, with little opposition from politicians and civil-society organizations who fear "the next Boko Haram."

Ultimately, John is concerned about the individual stories of people behind the headlines. In another interview, he notes that he writes fiction about realities that are "in danger of remaining in the shadows of two-minute news items about insurgent attacks." While his story may deal with violence and extremism—hot-button topics easy to be sensationalized by the media—it is also "the story of the human beings who get lost in big stories of insurgencies or humanitarian disasters and in the politics that gives birth to them."[18] Unlike media poverty porn,

John's writing goes beyond sensationalism to find the humanity in the stories beneath the headlines.

The photographs of Maiduguri-based photographer Fati Abubakar also provide an eye on life in the northeast beyond sensational headlines. She began by uploading scenes from everyday life in Maiduguri to Instagram, as well as images of people displaced by Boko Haram, photographs that she eventually put together in a traveling exhibition called "Bits of Borno." She told the *Daily Trust* that "the insurgency has been portrayed from mostly one angle, which is devastation and death. They [the media] don't really see outside of that, which is really unfortunate. And for the rest of your life, you will be labeled as something that came out of there, something that is depressed." In her academic work on the psychological health of refugees, she "discovered that despite the fact that there is a crisis going on, there are people outside of those that are affected that are resilient. They just group everybody as traumatised. But there are people that can bounce back and can become resilient. . . . So that was what I saw in Maiduguri and that was what I went for—the resilience." As opposed to photographs and journalism by outsiders, Abubakar's work focuses on portraying the everyday life of those who have survived the insurgency, what she calls "the good, the bad and the ugly."[19]

Imagining Boko Haram on Video

But while English speakers such as John and Abubakar have gained international attention for their work on the lived experiences of Boko Haram's victims, the most prolific storytellers of northern Nigeria are Hausa-language writers and filmmakers. The predominantly Muslim Hausa-language film industry, Kannywood, based primarily in the northern cities of Kano and Kaduna, represents nearly a third of Nigeria's overall industry, often known outside of Nigeria by the name of Nollywood. Like most Nollywood films, Kannywood movies are often shot and edited quickly and released on video, usually in multiple parts that resemble television serials more than cinematic features, although cinema releases are becoming more common. Stylistically, however, Hausa-language Kannywood films are quite different from their English-language counterparts. Most are interspersed with singing and dancing sequences inspired by Indian films. The most common plotlines are love stories and family dramas, although filmmakers also often tell stories inspired by personal experience or "true stories" read about in newspapers or heard through the rumor grapevine.

Because both the filmmakers and their audiences belong to conservative northern Nigerian Muslim communities, these films are generally more conservative than their southern relatives. Filmmakers and other northern entertainers also face a variety of formal rules and regulations designed to police their morality. For example, revealing costumes or portrayals of physical intimacy between men and women are banned. The films often have didactic, moralizing elements and frequently end with the punishment or confession and redemption of a sinner. But despite these elements, Kannywood filmmakers are nonetheless often scapegoated for what conservative critics see as the moral corruption of society. Only a few years before the Boko Haram crisis began, the Kano State Censorship Board had overseen the arrest and imprisonment of hundreds of people involved in the film industry, from film vendors and owners of viewing centers where audiences could watch the videos for a small fee, to editors, singers, and directors.

But while attacks by angry protestors and arrest by the state government had been bad enough, Boko Haram proved a far greater risk. Indeed, when we approached vendors about compilations of Boko Haram videos or films made about Boko Haram, they would often lower their voices or quickly protest that "they did not have anything like that." Likewise, when asking Hausa filmmakers as late as 2015 about whether they had plans to make films about Boko Haram, they told us there were many stories they would like to tell but that they felt it was not yet safe to make films about them. They were right to be cautious. Boko Haram was known for attacking its critics, and Mohammed Yusuf had critiqued the corruption of the film industry in several of his early sermons.

While Kannywood filmmakers felt that it was too risky to make films directly about Boko Haram, there were metaphoric responses in a genre of disaster and "historic" films. Such films became particularly popular in the 2010s, coinciding with the rise of Boko Haram. Fantasy storylines about apocalyptic disasters in a mythic past or imagined future enabled people to imagine agency in the face of disaster and death. One notable film of this genre was the two-part film *Hindu,* which won a Kannywood award for the best Hausa film of 2015. On the face of it, it is a reimagined folktale about a stubborn Hausa princess named Hindu who refuses to marry any of her suitors, designing ever more impossible tasks for them to fulfill. Eventually, her plan fails and, in a plot device common to a wide range of African and European folktales where independent women are punished with trickster husbands, she is forced to marry an unkempt sorcerer who takes her to his camp in the wilderness.

However, in the second part, Hindu finds that her new husband is married to dozens of other women, most of whom he has kidnapped. At night, he gathers the women and their children and tells them gruesome tales of war where men were slaughtered and women raped. In this film that is ostensibly set in a land far away and long ago, there are disguised references to the current Boko Haram crisis where women are abducted and mistreated. When Hindu's cruel husband says that he tells these stories of brutal murder to his children every night so that they do not "grow up with an element of sympathy," the situation echoes the techniques Boko Haram use to initiate child soldiers and an atmosphere in which dehumanizing violence enters into the canon of tales told in northern Nigeria. Yet in addition to portraying horrors that audiences in the north could identify as contemporary, the film also imagines the agency of women to fight against a threat that harnesses male authority to dominate women. Ultimately Hindu's maidservant uses her own sorcery to defeat Hindu's evil husband before she finally throws away her magical instruments to become a good Muslim.

The battle between the sorcerer and Hindu's maidservant overlaps with stories reported in Nigerian newspapers about groups fighting Boko Haram spiritually. In 2014, there were reports of Christians and Muslims organizing prayer vigils against the terrorists and online tabloid reports that an organization called the Witches and Wizards Association of Nigeria was "ready to wage total war on the insurgents and bring them to their knees."[20] Even the BBC reported stories that captive Boko Haram militants attested to snakes and bees attacking Boko Haram in the Sambisa Forest. They believed there was a "supernatural aspect to the attacks."[21] By harnessing rumors and headlines and reimagining them into storylines not directly related to Boko Haram, *Hindu* and other "disaster films" were able to imagine the trauma of displacement, death, and terror that large proportions of their audiences were facing. The films also, arguably, imagine solutions, without directly placing themselves in conflict with a terrorist group known to attack anyone who challenged it.

While Kannywood filmmakers initially avoided the topic of Boko Haram, Nollywood did occasionally make an effort to address it. One example is the 2013 *Nation under Siege,* one of several English-language Nollywood films that, Noah Tsika points out, "underscore the Afro-pessimist conception of a hopelessly divided Nigeria."[22] Although the film was initially named *Boko Haram* and remained so when it was screened in Ghana, the name was changed in Nigeria after it was refused cinema screening rights because of fears about the possible incendiary impact on audiences. The film portrays a terrorist who comes to Lagos as part of a plot to kill thousands of people but is partially dissuaded from his mission by a Christian prostitute. A security agent in the film claims that the terrorist group is "a group of immigrants occupying land in the far north." Such films seemed to merely reinforce southern stereotypes about the "foreign" nature of Islamic insurgency, where the threat comes from the north and the victims are from the south.

Other English-language productions were set in the north, with minor participation by northern actors, including Udoka Oyeka's short film about the ethical dilemma of a doctor who helps save the life of a wounded terrorist, *No Good Turn,* which went to several international film festivals in 2016. By 2017, Kannywood actors had become more involved in productions about Boko Haram. In June and July of 2017, an internationally sponsored English-language television series, *In Love and Ashes,* set in Maiduguri in the aftermath of Boko Haram and featuring a character based on photographer Fati Abubakar, was shot with Nollywood and Kannywood actors. Around the same time, the first widely advertised Hausa-language film about Boko Haram was shot when a Lagos-based production company featured several Kannywood stars in its production *Make Room.* And in 2017, the first actual Kannywood productions to deal with the conflict began to be released. Zahradeen Sani went through long negotiations with the National Film and Video Censors Board and the SSS before an October release of his film *Abu Hassan,* which dramatizes a military officer's fight to rescue his daughter who has been kidnapped by a terrorist group. Nasir Gwangwazo, a Kano-based scriptwriter and producer, wrote a script that addresses Boko Haram even more directly. In his film *Aliko,* a young man gets caught up in Boko Haram, and it is only when he sees one of his sister's friends abducted that he begins to repent. Gwangwazo told the Hausa newspaper *Rariya* that the weakening of Boko Haram made it possible to make a film about Abubakar Shekau, although at the time of writing, the film had not yet been released.

Although artists associated with Kannywood were initially cautious about how they spoke about Boko Haram in the early days of the insurgency, there were a surprising group of Hausa-language artists who responded more directly to Boko Haram: Christian musicians, many of them from northeastern states such as Adamawa or Taraba

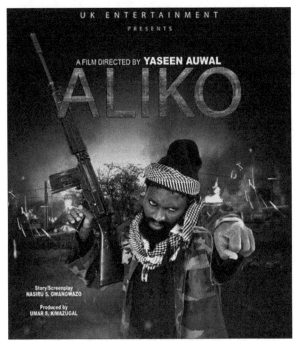

Figure 3. Promotional poster for *Aliko*, 2017 (produced by Umar S. K. Mazugul)

where there are large populations of Christians. These musicians are associated with production companies based in the Middle Belt city of Jos.

Songs about Boko Haram are sold on video CD albums that preach about Christian life and the trials Christians are currently passing through. The most striking aspects of the videos are the ways that they directly address both Boko Haram and its victims and the way that many of them call to a cosmopolitan unity between Christians and Muslims and between Nigerians and the rest of the world. That Christian musicians were quicker to respond directly to Boko Haram than Kannywood filmmakers probably says something about their more marginal nature in the mediascape of northern Nigeria—these musicians are not as regionally famous as Kannywood stars and therefore probably face less risk of universal recognition. Small-scale music video producers also generally avoid the time-consuming process of passing their albums through the National Film and Video Censors Board, which better-known film producers cannot avoid. Since many of them are from the northeast, there is also a feeling that they were already involved. A Christian music video producer, while not wanting to be identified by name, told us that musicians did not intend to insult the members of Boko Haram but rather to call them to repent. As such, these songs became part of their evangelistic mission as Christians.

Often these videos are in direct conversation—stylistically and in their content—with Boko Haram's own video propaganda. The Shekau faction's videos have long been dominated by its leader's monologues, often combined with footage of the group's military operations and executions. Featuring Hausa, Arabic, and Kanuri speakers and obviously intended to be viewed by Nigerian audiences, they are also sometime directly addressed (often by Shekau personally) to world leaders. Domestically the videos are distributed through Bluetooth phones, WhatsApp, and local "download centers," and they reach their international audiences via You-Tube and tabloid sites such as *Sahara Reporters.*

What is the goal of Boko Haram's media strategy? From the early days of Shekau's leadership, one emphasis has been on amplifying images already available locally that depict a Nigerian Muslim community under attack. These have included locally "viral" videos such as the one depicting Yusuf's interrogation and execution in 2009, or the video that showed Christian youth in Jos attacking an Izala group on the final day of Ramadan in 2011. They then respond to these injustices with media spectacles of their own. The "shock and awe" tactics of the attacks, whether suicide bombings or commando-style raids as happened during the 2012 attacks on Kano, draw on spectacles as diverse as the Hollywood action film, terror extravaganzas staged by al-Qaeda, and the global news aesthetics of embedded war journalists during the campaigns in Afghanistan and Iraq.

One of Boko Haram's most striking videos was released in March 2014 after attacks on Giwa Barracks in Borno. While much of the footage is set to a soundtrack of chanted Arabic verse originally produced by the Islamic State to encourage and commemorate its jihadist fighters, the soundtrack eventually transitions to poetry sung in Hausa that states Boko Haram's grievances, its intentions to kill "unbelievers" and destroy churches, and its appeals to "fellow Muslims" to join in the killing.[23] The music and poetry play over video images that show Boko Haram attacking the barracks with truck-mounted machine guns and rocket-powered grenades. The makers of the video present themselves as sympathetic heroes, showing people, including women in hijabs, running toward the camera as if to seek refuge with Boko Haram. The video's display of intimidating artillery draws from action-film tropes where the soldier is a liberator of passive, grateful populations, and it features spectacular explosions and shooting but without the chilling images of executions shown in other Boko Haram videos.

Local musicians, both Christian and Muslim, responded to this video and others by borrowing directly from Boko Haram's own images, confronting its members with evidence of their evil and warning them to repent. For example, Muslim rapper Bly opens his music video, uploaded to YouTube under the title "boko haram hottest song," with edited excerpts of Shekau's maniacal soliloquy—"Today our religion is killing, killing, killing. . . . Kill them. . . . Slaughter them"—intercut with images from Boko Haram footage of the terrorists slitting the necks of victims. With this opener, the musician begins his chorus in English: "We are crying because we are dying everyday. . . . You Muslims or Christians be united, we are one." Switching to a Hausa-language rap, he questions Boko Haram: "In the Qur'an which verse or hadith calls for you to kill Muslims your brothers?"

Christian music videos similarly juxtapose Shekau's words with his deeds to challenge Boko Haram's perceived ideology. Performers often use apocalyptic language, referencing scriptural narratives of God's judgment to make sense of the horror enacted by Boko Haram. Christian musicians draw on the New Testament's Book of Revelation, which speaks of the persecution of Christians and a series of disasters in the end of times before an eventual heavenly peace on earth. Both Muslim and Christian visual narratives invoke the final Day of Judgment as the punishment for injustice that goes unpunished on earth.

Brother Felix H. Phanuel Dong's album *Sun Ce Boko Haram* (They say education is forbidden), for example, cuts in clips from American evangelical films about the end of the world, showing buildings collapsing, flames raining down on earth, and spirits flying out of graveyards, alongside lyrics such as "You have been told in the Bible that the end of the world is near. . . . War everywhere, people's love has grown cold in this world, the end of the world is here."[24] In the singer Autan Zaki's song "Lokaci Ya yi" ("It is time"), he warns, "Believers it is time, we must wake from sleep. It is the end time." Indeed, almost all of these albums work as a kind of popular history and commentary on the end of the world, using documentary video footage of burned-out houses, military movement, news coverage of the Bring Back Our Girls protests, and footage of Boko Haram atrocities, passed around via Bluetooth and WhatsApp.

On his video album *Yan Chibok Ku Daina Kuka* (People of Chibok, dry your tears), the popular Christian performer Saviour Y. Inuwa addresses Shekau directly. Over video images of Shekau taken from Boko Haram propaganda videos, he sings, "Shekau, know that God's wrath is dangerous, come and repent when you still have the chance," while his backup singers respond, "Shekau, bring back our girls." Thus, the music videos become a way of both documenting the atrocities of Boko Haram and directly talking back at it.

Inuwa's is only one of a proliferation of songs that deal with the Chibok abductions, ranging from defiant to long-suffering. Ezra Jinang, for example, sings, "Let's go there! And bring back our girls" to a chorus of "Even though I walk through the Sambisa Forest, I shall not fear." Inuwa, on the other hand, attempts to comfort parents with such lyrics as "The coming of Jesus is at hand. Mama stop crying. Jesus will wipe your tears. Baba stop crying. God will wipe your tears." Others, like Sunday Bandi's album *Yanzu Mun Gane* (Now we understand), focus on the persecution of Christians. In the second track on Bandi's album, for example, he alternates a chorus that gives a litany of churches that have been burned with a chorus of dancing girls in hijabs singing, "Now, we understand this is a religious war."

While Bandi's albums fit in with the national rhetoric of CAN, remarkably a number of these songs fit more with the peacemaking efforts of Christian leaders like Bishop Kukah or Pastor Joseph Hayeb, promoting a unifying message built on a common Nigerian identity and the cultural elements that Christians and Muslims share. In many of the videos (even those that decry the persecution of Christians), Christian men and women dress in clothing generally seen as "Muslim": women with hijabs and men with long, white Saudi-style robes and kafiyyas. Yet they pair these costumes with crosses, praise songs to Isa (the Arabic name for Jesus), and clips from the 1979 *Jesus* film used in Christian evangelism.

In Helen Zakha Soja's album *Mutum Abin Tsoro* (Man is a fearful thing) that she performs with her husband, one of her songs is called "Hijira." Against photos of displacement camps, the Christian evangelist, wearing a hijab, compares the situation of IDPs to the Muslim hijra, singing, "We have left our homes and lands, here we are running for our lives."

In both costume and language, therefore, Christians appropriate the habits and communication devices of their Muslim neighbors, perhaps both consciously for

Figure 4. Evangelist Helen Zakha Soja, from music video for "Hijira"

dramatic effect and by long tradition of living alongside Muslims. And while there are evangelistic messages in many of the songs, there are also messages of unity in suffering. The chorus of the first song on Dong's album, for example, urges Christians and Muslims to pray together: "Disaster plague trouble has come to our land. It is called Boko Haram. Christians, let's pray for this our country. Muslims, pray for this country. Nigerians, pray for this country."

Similarly, Inuwa, dressed in a Saudi-style robe and kafiyya, opens the first song on *Yan Chibok Ku Daina Kuka* with a prayer: "Muslims and Christians in the whole of Nigeria, Lord, grant us peace and harmony amongst us." Later on, he takes the theme of religious unity even further by referencing Boko Haram's attacks on local Muslim traditional leaders, referring to them as "our" kings despite a long and contentious history of Christian resistance to accepting their authority. These expressions of interfaith community from both Christian and Muslim musicians in popular music videos suggests that despite the efforts of Boko Haram and the rash threats made by CAN representatives, there is a grassroots solidarity among many of those most at threat by Boko Haram.

Nor does this cooperation across religious boundaries stop at the grassroots level. In the same song, Inuwa poses a larger, cosmopolitan unity of global humanity opposed to Boko Haram's atrocities, singing over a montage of images that juxtapose world leaders and local and international Bring Back Our Girls demonstrations, "Was it only Nigeria that was worried? No, wait and listen. Not us alone." He adds that "the king of Mecca cried," along with Chad and France, while America, China, Cameroon, Ghana, and Israel also expressed their dismay. Here, he reaches out to African neighbors, to the leader of the symbolic home of Islam, and to Western and Eastern powers, drawing them into the sorrow of a subaltern Chibok. While international media coverage of the Chibok abductions sometimes seemed to value headlines over protecting their sources, Inuwa's song, and its documentary images of protests, indicates the symbolic power of the global solidarity brought about by the Bring Back Our Girls movement.

* * * *

As distinct from writing in English, which often seems concerned with demonstrating the humanity of the north against sensational representations by foreign and southern Nigerian media, these Hausa-language productions demonstrate a sort of aggressive self-confidence that local artists are being heard: by Boko Haram, whom they challenge, by fellow sojourners in a land of suffering to whom they direct comfort and succor, and even by the most powerful rulers in the world, whose condemnations of Boko Haram they appropriate for their own messages.

While Boko Haram magnified fault lines between north and south, Muslims and Christians, these forms of media by musicians whose homes were in the regions most affected by Boko Haram offer a counterbalance, demonstrating the ways in which Nigerians can come together. And, ultimately, these productions in Hausa at the grassroots level offer the most hope for reconciliation. Baptist pastor and CAN representative Joseph Hayeb argued at the 2017 Kaduna literary festival Kabafest that ordinary Nigerian Muslims and Christians have lived alongside each other for over a century. It is the political elite (and Boko Haram) who are the ones who are pulling them apart, he maintained. The problem is not the ordinary person, he told the gathered writers, but those who do not hear, or who ignore, what they are saying. In other words, paying attention to the voices beneath the international media's chronicle of events is crucial to understanding the story of Boko Haram. The crisis is not just a litany of bombings, attacks, and abductions but also a collection of a million personal stories told by people who suffer and who survive.

Conclusion

On March 10, 2017, Stephen O'Brien, the UN undersecretary-general for humanitarian affairs, testified before the Security Council about what he termed the largest and most complex set of global humanitarian crises since World War II. At its center were four distinct disasters, each with a unique history. South Sudan's hunger crisis was the result of decades of nearly continuous civil war and chronic underdevelopment, while in Somalia the absence of an effective central state for over twenty years combined with drought conditions to leave nearly a million and a half children at risk of starvation. In Yemen, a bloody civil war and Saudi Arabia's military intervention had crippled the country's ability to import food, creating a man-made food security emergency.

Over the years, each of these has earned an occasional mention in Western media outlets as a "forgotten" conflict, and deservedly so. For Somalia and South Sudan, the sheer length of their crises has allowed them to easily move off the global radar as new ones appeared, while Yemen's war was overshadowed by the Syrian and Iraqi battles with ISIS. The fourth conflict, however, was a more recent addition to the international community's list. Although the Nigerian government's war on Boko Haram was, by this point, nearly a decade old, its broader consequences were just now becoming clear. And unlike in these other hot spots, there were few existing humanitarian networks and resources for an international response to build on. While the Chibok abductions drew headlines and a temporary burst of online activism, and the group's relationship with global jihadist terrorist organizations attracted attention from policymakers in Western capitals, few had been prepared for the scope of the human tragedy that had unfolded across the Lake Chad region, particularly in northeastern Nigeria.

From an outsider's perspective, the scale of the Boko Haram crisis is hard to imagine. Nor do the statistics, as gruesome as they are, fully communicate the scope of its impact on the lives of ordinary Nigerians and their neighbors in Cameroon, Niger, and Chad. Estimates of the number of deaths as of early 2018 directly attributable to Boko Haram vary widely, from slightly more than twenty thousand to over one hundred thousand, and estimates of combatant casualties (not to mention civilian casualties inflicted by governmental forces) are even harder to pin down. At the height of the war in 2014 and 2015, UN estimates suggest that over two million people were forced to flee their homes, taken in by a combination of poorly staffed and supplied camps and (more often) by informal "host communities" that welcomed the displaced but soon saw their own resources taxed to the limit. And even as some began to return to their towns, villages, and farms to rebuild, the best estimates available in March 2018 counted roughly 10.7 million people in the region, mostly in Nigeria, in immediate need of aid, including access to food and medical care. With an estimated $9 billion in damage to infrastructure, losses in human capital, and economic activity forgone, the UN's Humanitarian Response Plan 2018 appeal of $1.58 billon is at best a drop in the bucket.

Not surprisingly, children (both boys and girls) have been among the hardest hit. The UN estimates that between 2009 and 2017 as many as eight thousand children were recruited or forced into service with Boko Haram, including as slaves and camp workers, intelligence gatherers, lookouts, and combatants. Thousands more served with the CJTF and other local vigilante forces, often in roles that put them directly in harm's way. In a country that already suffers from a greater number of school-aged children outside the educational system than any other in the world (roughly 10.5 million in 2017), the effect is likely to be a "lost generation" in the northeast.

Another of the conflict's underappreciated consequences has been its impact on the region's economy. As early as 2012 and 2013, when the Nigerian government first began to consider using a "state of emergency" declaration to clamp down on Boko Haram's movements and supplies, local farmers and traders were already confronting markets and long-standing cross-border trade routes that had been shut down by the violence. As farmers were unable to plant and harvest, food prices soared, while Boko Haram took advantage of the situation to offer financial incentives to locals in exchange for their cooperation. In a region already battered by the visible impact of climate change (Lake Chad has lost 90 percent of its water mass since 1963), even a strong national and international commitment to reinvesting in agriculture and other livelihoods may not be enough to restore impacted communities to what they once were.

In the midst of these challenges, where might we find solutions? Among Nigeria's powerbrokers, a military defeat that kills Boko Haram's leaders and destroys its capacity to engage in future violence is often seen as the only real path forward. And, indeed, the Nigerian government's funding for new military equipment has long surpassed its investments in the more ordinary work of providing services for those displaced by the conflict. There was no clearer illustration of these priorities than the Buhari administration's acquisition of twelve light attack aircraft from the United States at a cost of nearly $500 million—planes that, it was revealed in April 2018, will not even be delivered until 2020—while allocating a mere $147 million to the Presidential Committee on the North East, the administration's crown jewel program for providing direct aid to Boko Haram's victims.

International advocates and Western governments have been stronger voices on the importance of emphasizing socioeconomic development for the region's poorest and most vulnerable citizens than Nigeria's own government, and many have devoted considerable resources to these efforts. From 2015 to 2018, the US government provided Nigeria with over $300 million in humanitarian and development assistance earmarked for helping Boko Haram's victims and attacking the "drivers" of violent extremism, such as poverty, joblessness, and poor access to education. These goals are important, and if the aid ultimately reaches the most vulnerable communities, it will likely improve the lives of many people. Yet even this solution addresses only some of the issues that allowed Boko Haram to arise in the first place. What else is needed?

For one, so much of the violence, destruction, and loss of life and livelihood is the result of the Nigerian government's tragically ineffective response. The Yusufiyya is not the first community of Islamic revivalists and reformers to challenge the Nigerian government's corruption and poor governance, nor will it be the last. The question of whether or not Yusuf's movement, with its limited but real connections to the larger world of global jihad, would have inevitably turned to violence is unanswerable. What is more certain is that the pattern of tragic errors of judgment by Borno's (and Nigeria's) political leadership that led from Yusuf's early preaching career to the July 2009 showdown could have been prevented, had the will existed. Without apologizing for or justifying the beliefs of Yusuf and his successors, it is easy to believe that a political class more concerned with justice and less invested in preserving its own power might have led the men, women, and children who became Boko Haram down a different path.

Many among Boko Haram's leaders today are unlikely to be dissuaded from violence or disengaged from the group peacefully. Yet everything we know about how they operate and recruit across the region suggests that, even now, there is a real possibility for creating "off-ramps" for those who have been coerced or pressured into participating in violence. These efforts will require that the Nigerian government and military find local partners from among religious and community leaders and other nonstate actors to help restore the confidence that has been lost by so many in their government's commitment to their safety and well-being. And while it will not be a simple process, the security services will have to reckon with and acknowledge how their actions in places such as Giwa Barracks have fueled Boko Haram's membership. The failure to do so at best buries these grievances under the surface for a time, laying the groundwork for yet another insurgency in the future.

Similarly, while it is an unfair simplification of Yusuf's and Shekau's religious visions to say that they primarily preached against government corruption, the fact is that that their ability to identify the hypocrisy of Nigeria's ruling class played a crucial role in their movement's early success. There is a pressing need in Nigeria for both new local and national conversations that empower ordinary citizens to expect (and then receive) more from their governments and that hold public officials who violate the public trust accountable. This, perhaps more than anything, was the promise that helped President Buhari to victory in 2015, yet as of this writing there is little concrete evidence that his administration will meet them. Meanwhile, serious scandals surrounding the government's use of resources earmarked for defense and development in the northeast continue to erode public confidence in the possibility of real change.

Another sad legacy of the Boko Haram conflict that cannot be addressed by arms and aid alone is the division it has sowed among Nigerians. It is important to remember that, most of the time, Nigerians of different backgrounds live together peacefully and productively, sharing common concerns and aspirations. Yet Boko Haram (and the Nigerian government's response to it) has contributed to polarization in two important ways. The first is the group's own campaign of violence. Although the bulk of Boko Haram's victims have been Muslims, its targeting of Christians (particularly those from ethnic minorities) layers over a real and contentious history of interreligious violence in the region and one that has worsened since the country's return to electoral democracy in 1999. Both politicians and ordinary citizens have often unsurprisingly chosen to interpret Boko Haram's attacks in light of these established patterns, with the result being deepened suspicion between communities that are otherwise potential allies in the fight for peace.

One source of optimism is the local artistic and cultural response to Boko Haram's violence that we have chronicled here. Where others have found division, recrimination, and conflict, these musicians and filmmakers have often emphasized their history of coexistence and the possibility of common cause between Muslims and Christians in putting an end to Boko Haram's violence. This is also an area where quality leadership—political and religious—can and has played an important role in reducing tensions. At both the national and grassroots levels, growing levels of social and political violence since the 1999 transition have encouraged new voices and nongovernmental institutions for peacebuilding and promoting tolerance to step to the fore. Some, like the North East Intellectual Entrepreneurship Fellowship, a US-funded program that has mobilized support online to counter violent extremism with the hashtag #NotAnotherNigerian, have international support, while there are many other purely local efforts. Although they have not always succeeded in preventing reprisals or curtailing abuses by security forces, they are an important resource for Nigeria's peaceful future.

Despite these efforts, grievances fueled by inequalities in access to wealth, power, and information continue to inspire conspiracy theories that reframe Boko Haram's destruction as little more than another manifestation of the country's dysfunctional "politics as usual." These dynamics undermine confidence in "official" accounts of the violence and leave many Nigerians searching for the "real" culprits of Boko Haram's rise among communities they have been primed to fear and oppose. And, indeed, many southern Nigerians see criticism of the government's ineffective response to the conflict through the lens of their own grievances about historical inequalities in access to presidential leadership, questioning the need for the federal government to do more to help "those people up there" when there are pressing and long-ignored problems in their own communities as well.

For example, in southeastern Nigeria, a resurgent movement for independence led by the Indigenous Peoples of Biafra (IPOB) plays on claims of historic "northern" monopolization of federal power and reads Boko Haram not as a national disaster for many of the country's most vulnerable citizens but as a continuation of what they have long believed to be Muslim political dominance. Nnamdi Kanu, the founder and leader of IPOB, often highlighted attacks on churches by Boko Haram in his incendiary broadcasts on London-based "Radio Biafra," describing them as part of a Muslim/northern plot to hold on to power. At the 2015 World Igbo Congress in Los Angeles, Kanu linked his calls for Biafran secession to Boko Haram's violence, saying, "We need guns and we need bullets. . . . We know now that the best way to defend yourself is to be armed because Boko Haram is everywhere."[1]

Meanwhile, Muslims in the north read the government's ineffective response and its violence against civilians as an intentional neglect of their needs or, even worse, part of an anti-Muslim "plot." In mid-2017, several fringe organizations claiming to speak on behalf of "northern" interests threatened members of the Igbo ethnic community in northern cities with forcible expulsion. This was followed by the shadowy release of an anti-Igbo song sung in the style of popular Hausa music, which included conspiratorial accusations that Igbos in the north were "disguising as Boko Haram."[2] Such rhetoric is frighteningly reminiscent of the months leading up to the anti-Igbo pogroms across the north in 1966 that killed as many as thirty thousand civilians and helped set off the country's tragic civil war.

The simplest explanation for all of this is that the Nigerian government's reliance on violence as a problem-solving solution makes all sorts of conflicts worse. The communities that hold most strongly to these conspiracies often have real grievances and make legitimate demands for reforms to empower citizens, invest in economic and social development, and improve the quality and accountability of government. This is particularly clear in the case of longstanding—but recently much worsened—violence between Muslim, Fulani-ethnic pastoral cattle herders and Christian-majority farmers across much of Nigeria's Middle Belt region. Here, a combination of climate-change pressure, legacies of poor governance on issues of land rights and use, and the country's subnational citizenship laws, which assign special benefits and privileges to residents labeled as "indigenes," have created another yet another crisis, with a death toll in the thousands. Boko Haram has sought to capitalize on these deadly clashes between herders and farmers to advance its own cause, while others have attempted (with little evidence) to link the herders with Boko Haram as part of a broader plot to attack Christians and ethnic minorities. Yet those who pit Nigerian against Nigerian in a zero-sum conflict tinged with ethnic and religious resentments make the very violence they fear more likely.

What does the future hold? As of this writing, the military capacity of the various Boko Haram factions is indisputably weakened from what appears to have been its high point in 2014 and 2015. Yet perhaps the group's most important hallmark has been its flexibility in the face of changing circumstances. For example, on February 18, 2018, fighters allegedly affiliated with the al-Barnawi and Mamman Nur–led ISWAP faction kidnapped 111 girls from a secondary school in Dapchi, Yobe State. While the response from the Nigerian authorities followed the pattern established during the Chibok attacks—deny anything had happened, dissimulate about the gravity of the situation (including several false statements that the girls had been rescued), and eventually be forced to admit everything—ISWAP responded unexpectedly. At 3 a.m. on March 21, ISWAP militants arrived in Dapchi with nearly all of the abducted girls (five had died and one, a Christian, had refused to convert to Islam), freeing them to their families along with a stern warning that they should never go back to school.

Although the Buhari administration later acknowledged that their backchannel negotiations had played a role in ISWAP's decision—and Buhari himself denied paying a ransom—it seems clear that ISWAP's real goal was a local PR coup. Unlike the Chibok case, all but one of the abductees from Dapchi had been Muslims, and freeing them publicly (video footage of the celebrating community as ISWAP's fighters arrived with the girls soon made the rounds locally and in the international media) seems carefully intended to establish the group's reputation as less violent, more interested in improving the lives of local Muslims, and more powerful than Shekau's faction. That the one girl they did not return was Christian reinforced al-Barnawi's message that he had no quarrel with local Muslims. Indeed, reports in late April 2018 suggested that ISWAP had begun serious efforts to "re-brand" their insurgency as a source of stability and order, and to leverage this change more effectively (as IS itself once had in Iraq and Syria) as a source of revenue. These efforts included offering safe passage to traders and access to grazing land for local herders in exchange for payment to the group, as well as (allegedly) sending infiltrators into IDP camps to encourage residents to return to their homes and farms explicitly so that their activity could be taxed.[3] Although there remains little evidence that these efforts have rehabilitated the reputation of Islamist insurgency across the region, they represent a troubling trend that the Nigerian government seems ill-equipped to counter.

Similarly, the Nigerian government's frequent premature claims of victory have done little to assure the public that the violence will eventually come to an end, and those that have already (and those that hope to) return home face an uncertain path forward. The longer the conflict continues, the more likely it is that some communities will simply never be rebuilt, a change that will impact communities across the country. Meanwhile, reports of official corruption (one 2017 report claimed that as much as half of all official humanitarian aid was diverted before it could reach those in need), sexual violence, and hunger in the region's IDP camps demonstrate that the current alternatives do not work either.

Ultimately, and despite the slowly increasing prominence of the conflict in global circles, the cost of providing peace and security to northeastern Nigeria will not fall on the international community alone, nor can simply turning a greater number of international eyes toward the region ensure that "something is done." For those who care, the international press has provided many compelling, well-documented, and deeply human stories about Boko Haram's victims. But when faced with a seemingly ever-worsening set of interconnected humanitarian crises, is it any surprise that these stories alone cannot muster the will, the money, and the new ideas necessary to end the violence and rebuild what has been lost?

The challenges are great. What will be done with Boko Haram's least visible victims—those kidnapped and coerced into participation, or who chose to fight with Boko Haram in the face of few other options? The experience of the liberated Chibok abductees, who have seen their postcaptivity opportunities politicized as part of a national and international struggle over how to define the conflict, represents one aspect of the problem. But another is even more deceptively straightforward: What about those who want to go home? And what about those who fought on the side of the government, with the CJTF and others? Given the circumstances, new criticisms of government violence, corruption, and injustice are likely to emerge, and some will certainly be expressed in the language of Islam. Can they be addressed openly, or will the circumstances that led to Yusuf's rise and fall be repeated? And can a path forward that closes the gap between the "two Nigerias" finally be closed? There are no easy answers, and there will likely be more conflict before they can be resolved.

Notes

Introduction

1. Throughout this book, we will be using the name "Boko Haram" to refer to a variety of different groups that have emerged and split off from Yusuf's original movement, including the so-called Islamic State in West Africa (ISWAP). This choice reflects the colloquial usage in Nigeria. When discussing factions and splits by name, we adopt other terms as necessary.

2. Afua Hirsch, "Nigeria's Love of Champagne Takes Sales Growth to Second Highest in World," *Guardian,* May 8, 2013.

3. Chinua Achebe, *There Was a Country: A Personal History of Biafra* (New York: Penguin, 2012), 74.

Chapter 1: A Nigerian Origin Story

1. "Jihad" is one of the most complex and contested ideas in Islam. Literally translated as "struggle," the term is used in the Qu'ran to describe personal striving for piety and against temptations toward evil. As a 2002 Gallup survey found, this definition continues to resonate with many contemporary Muslims, who describe jihad simply as a "struggle to achieve a noble cause" or to fulfill one's "duty to God." It is also used to describe warfare, particularly against unbelievers, and it is this meaning that has dominated in classical Islamic scholarship and jurisprudence and that is most often referenced today. While we acknowledge the significance of this complexity to debates within Muslim communities, in this book the term

appears exclusively as used by groups and individuals discussing warfare in the name of their particular interpretation of the faith.

2. International Crisis Group, *Curbing Violence in Nigeria (II): The Boko Haram Insurgency,* Africa Report no. 216, April 3, 2014, 123.

3. Mercy Corps, "Gifts and Graft: How Boko Haram Uses Financial Services for Recruitment and Support," September 2016.

4. Hannah Hoechner, *Search for Knowledge and Recognition: Traditional Qur'anic Students in Kano, Nigeria* (Ibadan/Zaria: IFRA-Nigeria, 2013).

5. Mercy Corps, "Motivations and Empty Promises: Voices of Former Boko Haram Combatants and Nigerian Youth," April 16, 2016.

6. Institute for Economics and Peace, *Global Terrorism Index 2015: Measuring and Understanding the Impact of Terrorism,* November 15, 2015, 3.

7. "Shehu," roughly equivalent to the Arabic "Sheikh" (leader, learned scholar), is a common Muslim honorific in northern Nigeria and environs, as well as the title held by the kings of Borno since the early nineteenth century. It is also the term by which Usman dan Fodio is most widely known in the Sokoto Caliphate.

8. Murray Last, "From Dissent to Dissidence: The Genesis and Development of Reformist Islamic Groups in Northern Nigeria," in *Sects and Social Disorder: Muslim Identities and Conflict in Northern Nigeria,* ed. Abdul Rauf'a Mustapha (Suffolk, UK: James Currey, 2014), 25.

9. *Colonial Reports—Annual, Northern Nigeria Report for 1905–6, No. 516* (London: His Majesty's Stationery Office, 1907), 17.

10. Muhammad Sani Umar, *Islam and Colonialism: Intellectual Responses of Muslims in Northern Nigeria to British Colonial Rule* (Boston: Brill, 2006), 164–72.

11. Paul Newman, "The Etymology of Hausa *Boko,*" Mega-Chad Research Network (2013), http://www.megatchad.net/publications/Newman-2013-Etymology-of-Hausa-boko.pdf.

1. Andrew Walker, *"Eat the Heart of the Infidel": The Harrowing of Nigeria and the Rise of Boko Haram* (London: Hurst, 2016), 142–43.

2. Nick Tattersall, "Interview: Nigerian Sect Planned Bomb Attack during Ramadan," Reuters, August 4, 2009.

3. Mike Smith, *Boko Haram: Inside Nigeria's Unholy War* (London: I. B. Tauris, 2015), 83.

4. N. D. Danjibo, "Islamic Fundamentalism and Sectarian Violence: The 'Maitatsine' and 'Boko Haram' Crises in Northern Nigeria," Peace and Conflict Studies Programme, Institute of African Studies, University of Ibadan, 2009, 6.

5. Emmanuel Goujon and Aminu Abubakar, "Nigeria's 'Taliban' Plots Comeback from Hide-outs," Agence France-Presse, January 11, 2006.

6. Ahmed Salkida, "Boko Haram from the Beginning," *Sun* (Lagos), May 18, 2014 (originally printed in 2009).

7. Ibid.

8. Alexander Thurston, *Salafism in Nigeria: Islam, Preaching, and Politics* (New York: Cambridge University Press, 2016), 211–13.

9. Quoted in Anonymous, "The Popular Discourses of Salafi Radicalism and Salafi Counter-Radicalism in Nigeria: A Case Study of Boko Haram," *Journal of Religion in Africa* 42, no. 2 (2012): 136.

10. Alexander Thurston, "Nigeria's Mainstream Salafis between Boko Haram and the State," *Islamic Africa* 6, no. 1–2 (July 2015): 109–34.

11. Ahmed Salkida, "Muhammad Yusuf: Teaching and Preaching Controversy," *Sunday Trust,* March 1, 2009.

12. Translated and reprinted by Ahmed Salkida, ibid.

13. Translation of Hausa-language video transcription by Khadijah Gambo Hawaja, generously provided by Phil Ostien.

14. Ahmed Salkida, "Sect Leader Vows Revenge," *Daily Trust,* July 27, 2009.

15. Transcript in "Boko Haram, Mohammed Yusuf Being Interrogated before His Execution," *Sahara Reporters,* August 2, 2009.

16. Njadvara Musa, "Nigeria Police Claim Victory over Radical Sect," Associated Press, July 31, 2009.

17. Mayowa Tijani, "This Is Ahmad Salkida, the 'Wanted' Journalist Who Knows BH Inside and Out," *Cable*, August 15, 2016.

18. Habeeb Pindiga and Isa Umar Gusau, "Dead Boko Haram Leader Re-Emerges in New Video," *Daily Trust*, July 1, 2010.

19. Transcription and translation generously provided by Phil Ostien.

20. Ibid.

Chapter 3: A Nation in Crisis

1. Mike Smith, *Boko Haram: Inside Nigeria's Unholy War* (London: I. B. Tauris, 2015), 120–21.

2. Ahmed Salkida, "Revealed! The Suicide Bomber," *Blueprint*, June 26, 2011.

3. "How Nur, Shekau Run Boko Haram," *Vanguard*, September 3, 2011.

4. Ahmed Salkida, "Face of a UN Bomber," *Blueprint*, September 5, 2011.

5. Smith, *Boko Haram*, 122.

6. Jacob Zenn, "A Biography of Boko Haram and the *Bay'a* to Al-Baghdadi," *CTC Sentinal*, March 19, 2015.

7. Jacob Zenn, "Leadership Analysis of Boko Haram and Ansaru in Nigeria," *CTC Sentinal*, February 24, 2014.

8. Ibid.

9. "How Nur, Shekau Run Boko Haram," and "Kabiru Sokoto Names Boko Haram's Leaders," *Daily Post*, February 14, 2012.

10. John Campbell, "To Battle Boko Haram, Put Down Your Guns," *Foreign Affairs*, September 9, 2011.

11. NOI Polls, "The Boko Haram Sect and Insecurity in Nigeria," August 2011, and "Almost 3 in 10 Nigerians suggest Dialogue with the Boko Haram Sect," April 2013, both at www.noi-polls.com.

12. Amnesty International, *Stars on Their Shoulders, Blood on Their Hands: War Crimes Committed by the Nigerian Military*, June 2, 2015, 74.

13. Super Odomovo Afeno, "Killings by the Security Forces in Nigeria: Mapping and Trend Analysis (2006–2014)," in *Violence in Nigeria: A Qualitative and Quantitative Analysis,* ed. Marc-Antoine Pérouse de Montclos (Ibadan: IFRA Nigeria), 119–20. US data from US Bureau of Justice Statistics.

14. International Crisis Group, *Watchmen of Lake Chad: Vigilante Groups Fighting Boko Haram,* Africa Report no. 244, February 23, 2017, 12–13, 4–5.

15. Quoted in Eromo Egbe, "They're Defeating Boko Haram but Are They Nigeria's Next Security Threat?," IRIN, August 22, 2016.

16. Mia Bloom and Hilary Matfess, "Women as Symbols and Swords in Boko Haram's Terror," *Prism* 6, no. 1 (2016): 105–21.

17. Hilary Matfess, *Women and the War on Boko Haram: Wives, Weapons, Witnesses* (London: Zed Books, 2017), 136–39.

18. Jason Warner and Hilary Matfess, "Exploding Stereotypes: The Unexpected Operational and Demographic Characteristics of Boko Haram's Suicide Bombers," Combatting Terrorism Center, US Military Academy, August 9, 2017.

19. Matfess, *Women and the War on Boko Haram*, 126–30.

20. Isaac Abrak, "Boko Haram Leader Says Ruling Nigerian Town by Islamic Law," Reuters, August 25, 2014.

21. Mercy Corps, "Gifts and Graft: How Boko Haram Uses Financial Services for Recruitment and Support," September 2016.

22. Fulan Nasrullah, "3rd September 2014 Nigeria SITREP (Boko Haram)," *Fulan's SITREP* (blog), September 3, 2014, https://www.fulansitrep.wordpress.com/2014/09/03/3rd-september-3-14-nigeria-sitrep-boko-haram.

Chapter 4: A Tale of Two Countries

1. Fidelis Mac-Leva, Isiaka Wakili, and Hamza Idris, "Chibok: How Dame Patience Quizzed Borno Officials," *Daily Trust,* May 11, 2014.

2. "Nigeria Official Says She's Tired of Talking about the Kidnapped Girls," ABC News, May 10, 2014.

3. Megan R. Wilson, "Nigeria Hires PR for Boko Haram Fallout," *Hill,* June 26, 2014.

4. Goodluck Jonathan, "Nothing Is More Important Than Bringing Home Nigeria's Missing Girls," *Washington Post,* June 26, 2014.

5. Aminu Abubakar, "Boko Haram Seized 300 Children in Second 2014 School Attack: Locals, HRW," AFP, March 30, 2016.

6. Ayo Oritsejafor, "A Communique Issued by the Christian Association of Nigeria (CAN) in Response to the 2011 Christmas Day Bombing in Madalla, Jos, Damaturu and Maiduguri," *Weekly Trust,* December 31, 2011, 12.

7. Abubakar Shekau, "Declaration of War against Christians and Western Education," in *The Boko Haram Reader: From Nigerian Preachers to the Islamic State,* ed. Abdulbasit Kassim and Michael Nwankpa, trans. Abdulbasit Kassim (London: Hurst, 2018), text 23.

8. Marie-Therese Nanlong, "Boko Haram Killed over 8,000 Members of My Church—President," *Vanguard,* August 23, 2015; Zakariya Musa, "Church of the Brethren Loses Members in Boko Haram Attack," *Mennonite,* June 22, 2017.

9. Leonard Karshima Shilgba, "On Nigerian Elections and 'Christians,'" *Today's Challenge* 1, no. 2 (March/April 2015): 18–19.

10. Jay Loschky, "Nearly All Nigerians See Boko Haram as a Major Threat," Gallup News, July 9, 2014.

11. Adam Nossiter, "Chad Strongman Says Nigeria Is Absent in Fight against Boko Haram," *New York Times,* March 27, 2015.

12. Karin Barber, "Popular Reactions to the Petro-Naira," *Journal of Modern African Studies* 20, no. 3 (1982): 431–50.

13. Adaobi Tricia Nwaubani, "How to Protect the Chibok Girls from Reliving Their Horror," BBC News, October 29, 2016.

14. "Nigeria Boko Haram: Militants 'Technically' Defeated," BBC News, December 24, 2015.

Chapter 5: Who Speaks for Boko Haram's Victims?

1. Lanre Idowu, "Chibok and the Failure of Reporting," *Vanguard,* July 2, 2014.

2. Abdullahi Tasiu Abubakar, "Communicating Violence: The Media Strategies of Boko Haram," in *Africa's Media Image in the 21st Century: From the "Heart of Darkness" to "Africa Rising,"* ed. Mel Bunce, Suzanne Franks, and Christ Paterson (London: Routledge, 2017).

3. Rebecca Thomas, "214 Girls Kidnapped by Boko Haram Are Free Now—and Pregnant," MTV News, May 7, 2015.

4. Ludovica Iaccino, "Nigeria: Boko Haram Impregnated Girls 'to Guarantee New Generation of Fighters,'" *International Business Times,* May 6, 2015.

5. Christina Lamb, "Two Years Ago, the World Said #BringBackOur Girls. But What Happened Next?," *Sunday Times* (London), March 20, 2016.

6. Nicholas Kristof, "Is It Ever O.K. to Name Rape Victims?" *New York Times,* February 4, 2010.

7. Aryn Baker and Lynsey Addario, "The Secret War Crime: How Do You Ask Women to Relive Their Worst Nightmares," *Time,* March 10, 2016.

8. Dionne Searcey and Adam Ferguson, "Kidnapped as Schoolgirls by Boko Haram: Here They Are Now," *New York Times,* April 11, 2018.

9. Dionne Searcey, "Photographs of Dignity: How We Photographed Ex-Captives of Boko Haram," *New York Times,* April 11, 2018.

10. Chinua Achebe, "The Novelist as Teacher," in *Morning Yet on Creation Day* (Garden City, NY: Anchor, 1975), 42–45.

11. Binyavanga Wainaina, "How to Write about Africa," *Granta* 92 (2006).

12. Binyavanga Wainaina, "How to Write about Africa II: The Revenge," *Biodun* 21 (2010).

13. Ikhide Ikheloa, "The Caine Prize and Unintended Consequences," Pa Ikhide (blog), May 28, 2011, reposted March 11, 2012.

14. Mark Amaza, "Re-Introducing Northern Nigeria: Not as You Know It," Mark Amaza (blog), September 9, 2011.

15. Mark Amaza, "Living under Siege in Maiduguri," Nigerians Talk, April 11, 2012.

16. Carmen McCain, "The Caine Prize, the Tragic Continent, and the Politics of the Happy African Story," *Daily Trust*, May 12, 2012.

17. Funke Osae-Brown, "Elnathan John Talks 'Born on a Tuesday,'" *Luxury Reporter* 4 (March 2016): 8–9.

18. Jeanne-Marie Jackson, Nathan Suhr-Sytsma, and Elnathan John, "Interview with Elnathan John," *Research in African Literatures* 48, no. 2 (2017): 89–93.

19. "'I Had to Rebel to Photograph Life in Borno,'" *Daily Trust*, July 31, 2016.

20. Isaac Dachen, "Nigerian Witches Declare Total War on Boko Haram," *Pulse*, July 21, 2014.

21. "Snakes and Bees 'Flush Out' Boko Haram Fighters," BBC News, June 26, 2014.

22. Noah Tsika, "Nollywood News: African Screen Media at the Intersections of the Global and the Local," in Bunce, Franks, and Paterson, *Africa's Media Image*, 200–210.

23. Abdulbasit Kassim, "Introduction to the Study of Boko Haram's Hausa and Arabic Poetry," *Medium*, May 19, 2017.

24. Unless otherwise noted, the English translations of lyrics come from the subtitles.

Conclusion

1. Colin Freeman, "The Man Fighting for Independence of the West African Nation of Biafra. . . . from a Flat in Peckham," *Telegraph*, January 21, 2017.

2. "Audio and Transcript: Anti-Igbo Song in Hausa Language Now in Circulation," *Sahara Reporters*, August 5, 2017.

3. Paul Carsten and Ahmed Kingimi, "Islamic State Ally Stakes Out Territory around Lake Chad," Reuters, April 29, 2018.

Index